Managing negative emotions

How to deal with anger, anxiety, and irritation anywhere and anytime

Byron Neal

Contents

Introduction

Negative emotions, such as sadness, fear, and anger, are an essential part of our day-to-day lives, and most of the time, many of us struggle to deal with these emotions effectively. It's normal to experience negative emotions at work, school, or even at home. In twenty-four hours, you could experience a range of emotions—from becoming frustrated with the workload from your boss, becoming angry at a friend, experiencing fear of taking the next bold step on a project, or, even becoming excited about your son's academic success. But how we handle these feelings can go a long way in determining our level of success in relationships, business, and even in our social life, in general. Therefore, we must develop the ability to regulate our emotions. In other words, we might be tempted to act on what we feel right away, but that often doesn't fix the situation that caused the feelings to begin with.

Take this scenario: You are one of the new junior marketing agents hired three months ago. Your contract states that you must bring in an average of four new customers every month and an average of one new customer every week. Failure to do so could lead to the termination of your contract. Today is the beginning of the last week of the month, and you have yet to bring in any new customers. In fact, the possibility of bringing in a new customer at all this month seems unattainable. You're overwhelmed by your circumstances and exhausted from stress. Finally, you are tempted to give up. However, you need to understand that giving up doesn't necessarily take away the negative emotion you are feeling. In fact, it might make the situation much more complicated. To effectively manage a negative behavior, you need to study your emotions and understand how your feelings work. Then, apply psychological and behavioral techniques to help you put your negative emotions in check before they can escalate.

This book is filled with simple and practicable behavioral exercises, designed to help you overcome your negative emotions. Therefore, helping you regain control over the emotions that can affect your personal and professional relationships. The techniques and exercises provided in this book have been trusted by thousands of people who have applied these lessons in their lives and who have ultimately witnessed positive results. In short, this is why we have decided to publish this book, so that we can reach as many people as possible who need practical and simple solutions when it comes to controlling their negative emotions.

Sometimes, life can be difficult, and circumstances outside of your control can often derail you from your plans. But with the help of this book, you'll learn how to persevere, handle pressure, control your impulses, and ultimately manage emotional and psychological distress. Besides, through sheer tenacity and determination, the simple steps and methods in this book will also help you achieve more than you ever thought possible.

When you're going through emotional challenges, such as depression, anger, apathy, etc., it is essential to seek help. Otherwise, these negative emotions can worsen over time, and they may even negatively affect other areas of your life, such as your overall mental and physical health. Therefore, it is critical to understand the causes of your negative emotions, so that you can ultimately seek help in learning how to control them.

In reality, we all need help with managing our negative emotions. Therefore, take a bold, pro-active step by downloading this book now, in order to take control of your emotional state, so that you can start living a more positive and peaceful life.

Section No. 1. The origin of emotions

1.1 What are emotions?

External factors outside of our control can affect us in unpredictable ways. In fact, we decide to act in the presence of external threats or in response to our physiological needs. We each react to events in different ways, especially those that involve injustice and that go against our fundamental principles. There is always a force, however, that drives us to take act — our emotions. What are emotions?

Emotion is often defined in psychology as *a complicated state of feeling that results in physical and mental changes that influence thoughts and behaviors.* Human emotion involves the physiological arousal, conscious experience, and expressive behaviors of the individual. At a particular time, the emotional state of a man is associated with a range of psychological phenomena, which includes personality, temperament, motivation, and the mood of the individual.

Emotion is a heterogeneous, psychological phenomenon that encompasses a wide variety of significant mental and behavioral responses. Feelings are very subjective because they involve a particular person, object, or situation. Others, such as distress, joy, or depression, may appear to be very general in nature. Some emotions, such as a sudden flush of embarrassment or a burst of anger are very brief, while others, such as love or resentment may last a long time, until they eventually become a part of an individual's personality. Emotion may have pronounced physical or facial expression, or it may be invisible to outside observers. An emotion may be socially appropriate, inappropriate, or obligatory. For example, the feeling of grief at a funeral or the feeling of remorse after committing a crime is culturally appropriate. Interestingly enough, these emotions are different in their structure and their context. Psychologists believe these categories of emotion may not be part of a single class, but rather, they are best understood as a large family of loosely-related psychological phenomena.

Emotion can also be classified either as a state or as a process. When understood as a state, as in the state of anger or fear, an emotion is a type of mental state that connects with other mental states to cause precise external behaviors. On the other hand, emotion must be divided into two different parts before it can be understood as a process. The first part, also known as the *early part* of the emotion process, is the interaction between the individual's perception and their bodily response to that stimulus. The first part of the process includes an evaluation of the stimulus. This means the occurrence of an emotion depends on the individual's understanding of the stimulus. For example, an individual may react with anger when they are laid-off from a job, while another person may respond with joy or even excitement. Therefore, emotion depends on how the individual evaluates an event. The evaluative component in the process has shown that an emotion is not a direct or straightforward response to a stimulus. In this way, an emotion differs from a reflex – such as the startle response or the eye-blink response – which are immediate responses/reflexes to a particular stimulus. The second part of the emotion process is a body reaction, such as a change in heart rate or facial expression. However, this classification ignores some aspects of the process. These include the subjective awareness of the emotion and behavior that is often part of the emotional response, such as fighting or running away (aka, fight or flight).

For the sake of simplicity, emotion can be divided into those that are positive or negative. This classification, based on the qualities of a particular emotion, is called *affective valence*. But the complexities of emotion go beyond these opposing classifications. For example, love and hate are often considered contradictory emotions, yet they frequently coexist, and are not simply opposites, but rather complements. This is a phenomenon we must have witnessed at some point in our lives, and the plot structures of many movies and novels have only supported this. The classification of these emotions goes beyond their distinct characteristics. If we consider the features in the grouping or classification of these emotions, we may be ignoring several compelling factors. In other words, they are too complicated and often too subtle to be classified on this basis alone. More so, negative emotions (like anger) can be enlightening for an angry person, and when this emotion is expressed in the appropriate context, it can ultimately be beneficial.

According to Don Hockenberry and Sandra E. Hockenberry, an emotion is a complex psychological state that involves three distinct components: the subjective experience, the subject's physiological response, and finally, the subject's behavioral or expressive response.

In 1972, psychologist Paul Eckman, proposed six different types of emotions that are universal throughout human cultures, and they include the following:

- Fear
- Disgust
- Anger
- Surprise
- Happiness
- Sadness

Furthermore, in 1980, psychologist Robert Plutchik, introduced the *Wheel of Emotions* that works similar to an artist's color wheel. This is a new classification system for human emotion that shows how different emotions can be combined or mixed to form different feelings. This model is similar to how an artist mixes primary colors to create other, secondary colors. According to this theory, the primary emotions act like building blocks, and complicated emotions are therefore the result of a combination of the basic, primary emotions. For example, basic, primary emotions, such as joy and trust, can be combined to create a complex feeling, such as love.

Finally, in 1999, Eckman further expanded on the previous works of Paul Eckman and Robert Plutchik. Eckman's classification included several other basic emotions: embarrassment, contempt, shame, pride, excitement, amusement, and satisfaction.

Key Elements of Emotions

To better understand what emotions are, we need to focus on three of the essential elements:

1. The subjective experience.
2. The physiological response.
3. The behavioral response.

The Subjective Experience

It's true that regardless of our background or culture, everyone around the world experiences the same basic universal emotions. However, experiencing emotion can be highly subjective. Take anger, for example. All expression of anger isn't the same. A particular person's expression of anger may range from mild annoyance to blinding rage. While there are broad labels for emotions, such as anger, sadness, or happiness, every individual experience of these emotions is multi-dimensional, and therefore, subjective. In addition, we don't always experience pure forms of each of these emotions. In other words, people often experience mixed emotions over different events or situations. On the first day of a new job, you may feel both excited and nervous. Also, getting married, and eventually having children might be marked by a wide variety of emotions that may range from joy to anxiety. In most cases, these emotions simultaneously occur unintentionally, or you might feel them one after another.

The Physiological Response

Emotions can cause a robust physiological response, especially if you've ever been in a situation where your stomach has lurched from anxiety or your heart has pounded with fear. That is the reactive effect of emotions, which can cause intense physiological reactions. Also, this is a typical example of the Cannon-Bard theory of emotion, which explains how we feel emotions and experience physiological responses simultaneously.

The sympathetic nervous system controls involuntary responses in our body, such as blood flow and digestion. It also regulates many of the physiological reactions we experience during an emotional outburst. Physiological responses, such as sweaty palms or a racing heartbeat, are controlled by a branch of the autonomic nervous system. When facing a threat, fear, or any form of danger, these responses automatically prepare our body to run from the threat or fight the threat head-on. While early studies of the physiology of emotion focused on these autonomic responses, psychologists have since used this approach to explain our body's involuntary reaction to different emotions.

The Behavioral Response

This is the final element and perhaps the most important. People are more familiar with emotional and behavioral responses because they are regarded as the actual expression of emotion. The human behavioral intervention plays a significant part in our overall body language, especially when it comes to better understanding other people, and how they feel about us (e.g., in the case of lovers or business partners). We invest a lot of time interpreting the emotional expressions of the people around us. An individual's ability to accurately understand these dynamic expressions is tied to emotional intelligence. However, regardless of the culture, laws, or customs, some feelings are universal, such as a smile that indicates happiness or a frown that shows sadness. Socio-cultural values play a major role in how we express and interpret emotions. For instance, in the People's Republic of China, people tend to mask displays of fear or disgust towards their elders or other authority figures. Whereas, in Western cultures, like the United States and the United Kingdom, people are more likely to express negative emotions to anyone, including authority figures, within the limits of the law. Also, Chinese citizens are more likely to express displeasure alone, while their Western counterparts are more likely to express dissatisfaction towards others.

However, it is essential to note that the identification and classification, descriptions, and insights into the different types of emotions have changed over time.

Emotions vs. Moods

Emotion is one type of effect, while other types include: mood, temperament, and sensation, such as pain. It's pretty easy to confuse emotions with a mood in everyday language because most people often use the terms *emotions* and *moods* interchangeably. Still, there is a clear distinction between these two psychological concepts. How do they differ? Generally, emotion is often quite intense and short-lived. Even more, emotion may have a definite and identifiable cause.

For instance, you may disagree with a spouse over politics, entertainment, or even fashion style. In the moment, you might feel angry for a short period. On the other hand, a mood is usually less intense when compared with emotion, yet it's longer-lasting. In many cases, it is quite difficult to identify the specific cause of a mood. For instance, you might wake up on the wrong side of the bed and find yourself feeling miserable for several days without any clear or identifiable reason why you feel this way.

A properly developed emotion allows people to live fully and remain happy. Love, compassion, and respect are essential emotional ingredients for cooperative and interpersonal relationships. Emotion stimulates moral and immoral behaviors, and they also play an essential role in the brain's ability to interpret creativity. Feelings provoke the mind to appreciate the aesthetics of art and nature. There is no beauty without emotions. In addition, emotion with the help of our physical senses, determines an individual's basic processes of perception, which influence the way people interpret the world around them. At the same time, some emotions, such as negative emotions, can get out of control and damage an individual's personal and social relationships.

1.2 The origin of human emotions

Writing about the nature and origin of human emotion is challenging since emotion can be analyzed from many perspectives. Different theories of emotion explain the nature and origins of humans, and how we operate. On the one hand, emotions are the sophisticated and subtle epitome of what makes us human, and on the other hand, human emotions are evident in our responses. However, our choice of emotions and how we express them reflect our social environment, but it also seems likely that emotions were shaped by natural selection over time. These and other complexities make a comprehensive understanding of the nature of human emotion difficult. They have led to the creation of a variety of different theories in respect to this topic.

Theories about the nature of human emotion can be classified in terms of the context within which the explanation is built upon. The standard settings are evolutionary, social, and internal. First, evolutionary theories provide a historical analysis of human emotions, usually with a particular interest in explaining why humans have feelings, in general. Second, the social theories attempt to explain emotions as the products of cultures and societies, with a specific interest in the role of culture and society in developing our emotions. Finally, the internal is the final approach, and it seeks to describe the emotion process itself. This chapter is organized around these three critical categories and the main features of emotion, which will also be explained. Also, this chapter will further discuss the basic concepts that are associated with each theory.

Human emotions exert an incredibly powerful force on our behaviors. Strong emotion can make individuals act in a way they may not ordinarily act or, in contrast, avoid situations they usually enjoy doing. Why exactly do our emotions influence our behavior? Why do we have feelings? What is the nature of human emotion? Psychologists and philosophers have suggested different theories to explain the complexities behind the nature and history of our emotions.

Theories of Emotion

The major theories of emotion can be classified into three main categories: physiological, neurological, and cognitive theories.

1. *Physiological theory:* This suggests that various responses in the body are responsible for our emotions.

2. *Neurological theory:* This theory suggests that brain activity is responsible for our emotional reactions.

3. *Cognitive theory:* This theory argues that the human thought process and other mental actions are responsible for creating our emotions.

Evolutionary Theory of Emotion

Charles Darwin, an English naturalist, biologist, and geologist, suggested that emotion evolved because of its adaptive features, allowing humans and animals to survive and reproduce. People seek a mate and reproduce because they have a feeling of love and affection for each other. Whereas, feelings of fear compel people to defend themselves or flee the source of danger. Darwin's evolutionary theory of emotion states that our emotions exist because they serve an adaptive role. People's emotions stimulate them to respond quickly to stimuli in their environment. This adaptive feature will help them improve their chances of success and survival. The ability to understand other human and animals' emotions could protect people from harm and ultimately aid in survival. When walking on the road, if you encounter a barking dog, chances are you will quickly realize that the dog is defensive and leave it alone. People can live peacefully and in harmony with other people and animals if we can correctly interpret the emotional displays of the people and animals in our surroundings.

The James-Lange Theory of Emotion

The James-Lange theory of emotion is one of the most famous examples of the physiological hypothesis of emotion. This suggests that emotions occur as a result of physiological reactions to events. This theory was proposed by psychologist William James and physiologist Carl Lange, which indicates that the way we see or perceive external stimuli would lead to a physiological reaction. This means our emotional responses depend on how we interpret physical reactions. For example, suppose you're on a camping trip with your colleagues from school, and you missed the road, and now you're alone in the woods trying to find your way out. While walking, you hear a sound behind you. It's a bear! You're scared and begin to tremble. All you can do is stand there while looking at the bear, but your heart begins to race faster, and now you're sweating. Based on the above scenario, this theory proposes that you'll conclude that you're frightened. In the moment, you may even think, *I am trembling, my heart's beating faster, and I'm sweating. Therefore, I'm afraid.* Still using the above scenario, The James-Lange theory of emotion, claims you are trembling, sweating, and your heart is beating faster because you are, in fact, frightened. This theory also suggests that the psychological and physical experience occurs one after the other. Therefore, you feel terrified because you are trembling, sweating, and your heart is beating faster.

The Cannon-Bard Theory of Emotion

The Cannon-Bard theory was first proposed in the 1920s, and his work was made famous by physiologist Philip Bard during the 1930s. The Cannon-Bard theory of emotion is another popular physiological theory. Although both methods made use of the physiological approach, Walter Cannon discarded the James-Lange theory of emotion. He pointed out several flaws that made the James-Lange theory baseless. In other words, he suggested individuals can experience these physiological reactions, such as the trembling of the body, sweating, and a faster heartbeat without necessarily feeling those emotions. For example, you might sweat, and your heart might race faster because you have been exercising, and *not* because you are afraid. Cannon further argued that emotional responses occur much faster and must be classified as a product of a physical state. When you encounter danger in the environment, your first instinct is fear before you start to experience the physical symptoms associated with anxiety, such as trembling, sweating, a racing heartbeat, and rapid breathing. According to the Cannon-Bard theory of emotion, our emotions along with our physiological reactions, such as a racing heartbeat, sweating, trembling, and muscle tension all coincide.

More specifically, the Cannon-Bard theory proposes that emotions are a result of an exchange of messages between the thalamus and other parts of the brain. That is, in response to the stimulus, the thalamus sends a message, and the transaction will result in a physiological reaction. Consequently, the brain also receives a stimulus, which then triggers an emotional experience. Unlike the James-Lange theory of emotion, the Cannon-Bard theory suggests that the psychological and physical experience of emotion at any point in time happens simultaneously. That is, one does not cause the other.

The Schachter-Singer Theory

The Schachter-Singer theory is also known as the *Two-Factor theory of emotion*, and it is also an example of a cognitive theory of emotion. This theory is the fusion of both the James-Lange theory of emotion and the Cannon-Bard theory of emotion, and it suggests that a physiological stimulation occurs first, followed by the individual's identification of the cause of the experience, which would be labeled as an emotion. In a threatening situation, an individual's stimulus leads to a physiological response that is then cognitively interpreted and labeled as an *emotion*. The Schachter-Singer theory draws on both the James-Lange theory and the Cannon-Bard theory. Like the James-Lange theory, this theory proposes that people form emotions based on physiological responses. An essential factor for labeling that emotion under this theory is the *context in which they occur*. It also suggests that similar physiological responses can produce different emotions. For example, you could experience the same emotion in two different contexts. First, you could experience a racing heart and sweaty palms during an important exam, and identify the feeling as anxiety. However, if you experience the same physical responses on a romantic first date, you might interpret those responses as love, affection, or even arousal.

Cognitive Appraisal Theory

The Cognitive Appraisal theory is also known as the Lazarus theory of emotion. This theory suggests that thinking must occur first before experiencing emotion. According to this theory, three sequences of events must occur before we can arrive at a feeling. The first sequence of events involves a stimulus, followed by thoughts that lead to the simultaneous experience of a physiological response and emotion. For example, if you encounter a wild animal in the woods, you will immediately think that you are in great danger. These thoughts will then lead to the emotional experience of fear, along with physical reactions, such as sweating, running, or a racing heartbeat.

Facial-Feedback Theory of Emotion

The Facial-Feedback theory of emotion suggests that our facial expressions are linked to our current feelings or the emotions we are experiencing in that moment. Charles Darwin and William James both used this theory to show the direct relationship between physiological responses and emotion, rather than dismissing a physiological response as merely a consequence of an emotion. Some psychologists who support this theory suggest that emotions are directly tied to changes in facial expressions. For instance, people who are forced to smile before taking a picture at a social function will look better in the picture and also have a better time at the event than they would if they had frowned all throughout the event.

Even though emotions can either positively or negatively influence the decisions we make and the way we see the world around us, there is still a lot of mystery surrounding the nature and origin of human emotions. Research on emotions continues to explore the factors responsible for our feelings and how they ultimately affect us.

1.3 Types of emotions

◆ Fear

◆ Anger

◆ Irritation

◆ Disgust

Different types of emotions influence how we live and interact with others. Sometimes it may appear these emotions determine how we live our lives. Our choices, actions, and perceptions are all influenced by our feelings at any given moment. In an effort to comprehensively explain the influence of our emotions on our lives, psychologists have tried to identify the different array of emotions that we experience. Various theories have emerged to categorize and explain the feelings experience, but for the sake of simplicity, this chapter will be focusing on psychologist Paul Eckman's six different basic types of emotions.

Basic Emotions

In the 1970s, psychologist Paul Eckman proposed six basic emotions that he suggested were universal experiences throughout every culture. The emotions he proposed include: happiness, fear, disgust, surprise, sadness, and anger. He later expanded his list of basic emotions to include: shame, pride, excitement, and embarrassment.

Let's take a look at some of Eckman's basic emotions and explore their impact on human behavior.

Fear

This is a powerful emotion that can also play an essential role in survival. Fear is an emotional response to an immediate threat. The sight of a fast-approaching car, a spider crawling on one's leg, or the possibility of being robbed while walking alone in the dark can cause fear. Fear is the primary emotion caused by threats to an individual or their environment. When faced with danger, your body naturally reacts. For instance, you may experience tense muscles, an increase in your respiration and heart rate, and your mind may even become more alert, preparing your body to run from the danger or stand and fight it. This physical response is a psychological reaction known as the *fight or flight response*. When you encounter or think about things that can hurt you, you have the urge to avoid them or get away from the threat altogether.

The idea that *negative possibilities characterize fear* center on the premise that emotions are always about things that have yet to happen, but may likely happen. There are many types of threats that cause fear, and they include:

- The danger of getting hurt, such as the fear of being hit by a speeding car while walking on the roadside.
- The threat of financial or material loss, such as the fear of losing your house to foreclosure or losing your job during an economic recession.
- The fear of making a fool of yourself or making a faux-pas (e.g., the fear of not talking during a board meeting or while you're on a date) because you don't want to say the wrong thing.
- The fear of losing the connection you share with people (i.e. in a romantic relationship or in a friendship), such as being afraid to confront a spouse or friend about their bad behavior
- The fear of hurting others (e.g., the fear of handling a baby).

In a sense, fear is a response to the possibility of getting into a situation that may cause any other emotions in this classification (e.g., fear of danger, fear of embarrassment, fear of loneliness, fear of disgust, and so on).

People who experience fear are often pre-occupied with knowing the source of their anxiety and the possible ways to avoid or escape the situation. For example, a person experiencing an immediate or physical threat may step back or even walk away from the situation. A person faced with a social threat, such as the fear of losing their job, may become more cautious and conservative in their actions and thought processes.

This response helps us deal with threats in our immediate environment. The physical response or expression to *fear* can include:

- *Physiological reactions:* sweating, rapid breathing, and a racing heartbeat
- *Facial expressions:* dimming or widening the eyes and pulling back the chin
- *Body language:* shaking, attempts to fight, or run from the threat

The way we express fear is subjective. In other words, we all don't experience fear in the same way. Some people are more aware of fear in specific situations. Also, this emotion is more likely to be triggered by objects. Sometimes, in the absence of fear, people can also develop a similar reaction to anticipated threats or even thoughts about potential dangers. This thought process is known as *social anxiety*, which involves an anticipated fear of a social situation.

In contrast, others purposely seek out fear-provoking situations. An amateur surfer or a journalist posted to one of the deadliest regions in the world, for example, are more likely to experience anxiety. Extreme sports and other thrills can be fear-inducing, but some people seem to thrive and even enjoy these situations. However, repeated exposure to these fearful scenarios (e.g., extreme surfing or news reporting) can lead to acclimation, which will reduce anxiety in the long run. This is the foundational basis of psychological therapy. During a therapy session, a patient is often exposed to their fears in a controlled and safe manner. Over time, due to acclimation, the feeling of anxiety or fear will begin to decline.

A competent fear system and its functional value is important for each of us. Our fear systems prevent us from getting into danger, and if we are already in a dangerous situation, our system will help us make the best choices on how to survive. However, people with phobias can be taught how to deliberately set off or slow down their fear system if a physician feels they are unnecessarily hyper-paranoid about things. For instance, people with Alektorophobia "the fear of birds" or Geliophobia "the fear of laughter" have a dysfunctional fear system and may be required to go through some psychological therapy to help them reduce or turn off their fear system.

Anger

Like fear, anger is a powerful emotion that plays a part in our body's fight-or-flight system. Anger is characterized by feelings of agitation, irritation, hostility, frustration, and antagonism towards others or a particular situation. When a threatening situation generates feelings of anger, you may have to avoid this and protect yourself by walking away, or by showing extreme compassion. Anger is often displayed through:

- *Body language:* using strong language, fighting, shaking, or turning away
- *Facial expressions:* by grimacing, frowning, or looking directly at someone
- *Tone of voice:* crying, yelling, or shouting
- *Physiological responses:* sweating, experiencing a headache, or turning red
- *Aggressive behaviors:* hitting/punching, throwing objects, or fighting

Although anger is often seen as a negative emotion, it can sometimes be a good thing. When used in the right circumstance, it can be constructive. For instance, it can help you clarify or better express your need in a social or relationship setting. It can also build your momentum to take action and find solutions to things that are bothering you. However, anger becomes a psychological problem when it is excessive or expressed in an unhealthy, dangerous, or otherwise harmful way. Unchecked anger can turn into aggression, abuse, or violence. In addition, unchecked anger can make it difficult to make rational decisions and can even have a negative impact on your physical health. Medical researchers have linked anger with the onset of diabetes and coronary heart disease. This emotion can have both mental and physical consequences, such as aggressive driving, excessive alcohol consumption, and smoking.

Disgust

Disgust is a strong feeling of dislike for something that has a very unpleasant appearance, smell, or taste. Disgust is one of the original six basic emotions described by Eckman. When disgusted, people show it in the following ways:

- *Facial expressions*: lowering the eyebrows, wrinkling on the side and bridge of the nose, raising the upper lip in an inverted "U" shape, raising, and slightly protruding the lower lip.
- *Body language*: moving away or getting rid of the object of disgust.
- *Physical reactions:* nausea or retching.

Disgust is often a reaction to several things at the same time, such as an unpleasant taste, sight, or smell. For example, when people are told about a barbaric act, or the smell or taste foods that have gone bad, their usual reaction is disgust. Medical researchers believe this emotion, in most cases, is a reaction to the body's way of avoiding things that may carry transmittable diseases, such as food that may be harmful to our health. Other causes of disgust may include: poor hygiene, a strong smell, infection, blood, rot, and death. Also, people can experience *moral disgust* when they're told about a distasteful, cruel, evil, or immoral act or witness others engaging in such actions.

Sadness

Sadness is a short-lived emotional state that is affected by or expressive of grief, disappointment, hopelessness, unhappiness, disinterest, or a dampened mood, in general.

Like other emotions, we've all experienced sadness at some point in our lives. However, the duration of this state varies. In some cases, a prolonged and severe period of sadness can lead to depression. People can experience sadness in several ways, including:

◆ Crying
◆ A dampened mood
◆ Lack of energy or interest
◆ Silence
◆ Indifference
◆ Withdrawal from others

The root cause of sadness determines its severity, and how people cope with this feeling can also vary drastically. To deal with sadness, people may decide to avoid their friends and family, ruminate on a negative thought, or even self-medicate. These behaviors can often further exacerbate and even prolong the feeling of sadness rather than stopping it altogether.

Section No. 2. Factors that affect emotions

2.1 How sleep affects mood

Have you ever woken up early so you could beat rush-hour traffic? But throughout the rest of the day, you experienced a profound case of a *bad-night feeling*. Fortunately, you were able to beat the traffic and arrive at work early, however, you feel tired, irritable, and are struggling with an overall malaise that comes with the start of a new workweek. Although it's important to beat the rush-hour traffic, it's more important to get enough rest. Adequate sleep is vital for our well-being. When we sleep, we give our body enough strength to support brain function and maintain good physical health. When you don't get enough sleep, you feel tired, grumpy, and may find it difficult to concentrate on things. A lack of sleep can also affect your judgment and coordination. Still, similar to the cognitive impact of a lack of sleep, most people don't realize how deeply sleep deprivation, especially over a long period of time, can harm their emotional state, mental health, outlook, performance, and personal and professional relationships.

A lack of sleep can make you act in a way you normally never would. Due to inadequate sleep, you could, for example, uncharacteristically snap at a friend or family member over some minor issue. I don't need to tell you that poor sleeping habits can make you angry and short-tempered. We all know, through experience, how inadequate sleep puts us on a short fuse. Both in the short and long run, the amount of sleep we get can have a significant impact on our mood and overall mental health. Just one night of insufficient sleep can cause severe stress and frustration, which can change your attitude for the entire day. Chronic sleep deprivation can have profound effects, significantly affecting your overall mood and even leading to health challenges, such as depression and anxiety. The impact of sleep on our mood is an important and complex topic that requires more research for a comprehensive understanding. However, the little we do know about the relationship between sleep and mood indicates that rest, in general, is a critical part of our physical and emotional well-being.

In this chapter, we'll go into a panoramic explanation of what is known about sleep, mood, and mental well-being. We'll also discuss how you can use sleep to help you overcome negative emotions and brighten up your mood.

Finally, we will also provide sleep-aid methods that experts agree can help facilitate your sleep and make you feel healthy, happy, and well-rested.

Sleep and moods

A mood is a general or specific emotional state. For example, at the beginning of the day, a person may be in a positive and uplifting mood, yet, at the same time, experience a mood marked by sadness or anger. The quality of sleep you get can affect both your general and specific mood. The lack of quality sleep can contribute to a negative mood. On the other hand, getting quality sleep can contribute to a happier and more positive mood. It's important to note, the influence of sleep on mood isn't just about how much sleep we get, although the quantity of sleep is essential. The quality of sleep is much more important. If your sleep is broken/intermittent, or even too short, there is a chance that you won't experience the same benefits to your mood as someone who has fewer interruptions and smooth progressions during their sleep cycle (even if you both get the same amount of sleep).

One bad night or a sleepless night is enough to change your mood for the rest of the day. Think about how one night of bad sleep can make you feel the next day. For many of us, we're grumpy and angry. We find it difficult to concentrate, and we have no energy. It is easy to see how just one sleepless night can be a problem. It becomes even more worrisome, however, when an individual is suffering from long-term sleep deficiency. Long-term sleep deficiency can increase an individual's risk of serious psychological and physical health issues, such as heart disease, type 2 diabetes, and depression.

"Sleep is the best medicine."

~Dalai Lama

Sleep deprivation and mood disorders are closely related. In other words, they share a bipolar relationship. This means a lack of sleep can affect your mood, and your mood can also change your ability to sleep. Research has shown that people who sleep less are more likely to exhibit negative emotions, such as anger, frustration, irritability, sadness, in addition to a decrease in positive moods than people who have enough sleep. Besides, sleep deprivation is also one of the symptoms of a mood disorder, such as depression and anxiety. It can either raise the risk or contribute to the development of other mood disorders. Your sleep is also affected by your mood. In other words, when you experience anxiety or distress, your body reacts by keeping you agitated, and this constant agitation will make you sleepless. Even more, it will keep your body aroused, awake, and alert. You might discover you can't turn off your brain, and that your heart beats faster. So, getting enough sleep is essential to avoid the risk of damage to your overall physical and mental health.

The Impact of Sleepiness on Mood and Mental Health

> "I love sleep. My life has a tendency to fall apart when I'm awake, you know?"
>
> *~Ernest Hemingway*

Poor sleeping habits can alter your mood significantly. A sleep-deprived person is more likely to sit in a traffic jam and be combative with other drivers. They are also less likely to exercise, eat healthy, engage in fun activities, and even have sex. Aside from its clear impact on your physical health, poor sleep also affects your mental health. When you don't get quality sleep, your outlook on life, momentum, and emotions can be affected. When you feel low or down, it might be interesting to know that the lack of sleep is the culprit.

The relationship between sleep and mood is complicated because a lack of sleep can cause emotional changes, clinical depression, anxiety, and other psychological conditions. However, these conditions can also further disrupt sleep. Besides, disruptive sleeping patterns are the emblem of many mental health issues. We're still learning about the connection between sleep and emotion. But we know sleep deprivation affects the intricate emotional part of the brain, which makes us react or lash out in anger and frustration. If you find yourself sleeping late or too much regularly, it's essential to notify your doctor.

John just received a promotion at work, and his new job description requires him to be at work before everyone and leave after everyone. He wakes up early every morning and sleeps very late at night. At home, he often gets into a fight with his wife and loses his cool with his children. Similarly, at work, he snaps at his co-workers. He feels terrible each time he does this, but he doesn't know the cause of his sudden mood change, much less how he can change it.

Poor sleep affects the amygdala

Sleep deprivation can contribute to an impulsive and intense emotional response in any given situation. These situations are almost never fun, nor do they lead to healthier or happier relationships. But emotional reaction goes beyond just being cranky. A sleepless night can make us react strongly or impulsively in certain situations. When suffering from a constant lack of sleep, as any other busy adult, you increase your chances of developing mental health issues. Sleep deprivation increases activity in the emotional rapid response center of the brain's *amygdala*. The emotional rapid response part of the brain controls many of our quick emotional reactions. When we don't get enough sleep, this part of the brain goes into overdrive, causing us to be more intensely reactive to situations. The effect of poor sleep on the amygdala isn't limited to negative emotions alone (e.g., anger and fear), but it extends across a broad spectrum of emotions.

Poor sleep affects the prefrontal cortex

Interestingly enough, a lack of sleep also affects the part of the brain known as the *prefrontal cortex*. The prefrontal cortex regulates the activities of the amygdala. In other words, it acts as the traffic cop for our emotions. When the lack of sleep forces the amygdala into overdrive, the prefrontal cortex is responsible for regulating the amygdala's ability to react in an extreme or excessive way. For example, when you are angry, the prefrontal cortex sees the anger as an impulsive reaction and tries to make you realize you're reacting too fast, and you should slow down. However, the lack of sleep makes the prefrontal cortex redundant, and as a result, you become more impulsive and less thoughtful of your other emotional responses.

Poor sleep affects the REM function

Regardless of our culture, gender, or height, we all endure emotionally-charged experiences on a daily basis. These experiences are stored in the brain as memories, and getting enough sleep is essential to processing them. REM sleep helps your brain process painful and difficult memories. This process also helps ease the emotional sting that comes with these memories. It also helps your emotional mind return to a neutral state. This nightly, emotional *reset* is essential for your overall mental health. REM sleep occurs during a typical night's sleep. When you sleep well, it helps the episodes of REM last longer. But when you don't get enough sleep or when your sleep is interrupted, REM can't reset your memories.

You have a more negative outlook

Sleep significantly affects our emotional brain centers. So, it is not difficult to imagine how a lack of sleep can contribute to a more negative mindset. The lack of sleep makes us focus more on the negatives, while also increasing the possibility of repetitive negative thinking. Repetitive negative thoughts are intrusive, difficult to control, and can significantly impact how you feel and function. Negative repetitive thoughts can also lead to the development of depression, a mood disorder, or anxiety. People with a sleep disorder have more repetitive negative thoughts and are less able to control their minds from thinking about negative things. Scientists have also discovered that the less sleep a person gets, the more difficult it can be for them to ignore thinking about negative feelings, thoughts, and experiences. Nobody wants to be trapped in their negative thoughts, but when you are sleep deprived, that's what happens, and it can be a difficult cycle to break.

> "I feel like sleep is the most important thing. I notice in my body when I don't get enough sleep on a constant basis, how I am dreary, or my mood changes, or I'm not as focused."
>
> ~D'Brickashaw Ferguson

You Worry More About the Future

A lack of sleep has a negative impact on our emotional reactions and fear responses, which can create a negative outlook, while, at the same time, making us worry even more. When sleep-deprived, we worry more about the future, especially if we are generally prone to worry. So, if you worry a lot, it's essential to get enough rest to maintain a healthy emotional balance, so that you avoid health problems. The lack of sleep increases anticipatory anxiety and aggravates the brain's worry response, contributing to anxiety disorders, etc. The brain activity of a sleep-deprived individual is much higher than a person who gets enough sleep. Therefore, this activity in the brain's emotional control center, further contributes to increased anxiety about the future.

"Sleep helps you win at life."

~ Amy Poehler

How Does Sleep Affect Emotional Reactivity?

Emotional reactivity is a situation in which you may find it difficult to control your emotional reaction. Emotional reactivity is exhibited through lashing out, feeling hurt, outbursts, withdrawing, or a limited ability to manage a response to an emotional stimulus. While some people see emotional reactivity as a negative behavior, others see these traits as defensive approaches or how someone may rebound when confronted with a difficult emotional situation. Some amount of emotional reactivity is good, but a lack of sleep makes the control of our emotions much more difficult. In short, our mood (and other mental processes, in general) can be negatively impacted by poor sleep.

> "While sleep is clearly vital to emotional well-being, what is it, exactly, about sleep that is so necessary? As it turns out, the mood disorder is strongly linked to abnormal patterns of dreaming."

> ~Andrew Weil

Sleep and Depression

Depression is a complicated psychological condition that can include many symptoms, such as feelings of sadness, a lack of energy, limited concentration, insomnia, and others. Many of the symptoms of depression can appear even more strongly and frequently when an individual isn't getting enough sleep. It's not true that everyone who has sleeping issues is depressed. However, studies have shown that a lot of people who experience sleeping problems are suffering from depression, and insomnia tends to amplify the symptoms of depression.

How can you Improve your Mood with Sleep?

It has been established that sleeping has a significant of influence on our mood and our mental health. Most of us try our best to get the right quality and quantity of sleep. Below are the best possible ways to get a good night's sleep and how you can ultimately use rest to manage your negative thoughts.

It Helps to get Help

Although most of the steps you need to take to improve your mood and overall mental health with sleep is in your hands, this process can be facilitated or enhanced when you work with a trained professional. Working with a counselor or psychiatrist can beneficial in many ways. Cognitive-behavioral therapy for insomnia (CBT-I) can reduce the extent of many mental health problems, and it can also reduce insomnia. This therapy procedure also helps combat issues like anxiety or depression and their impact on sleep.

Improving Sleep Through Sleep Hygiene

Cultivating the right sleeping habit will not only help you with your physical health, but it will also help with your mental health. Sleep research has indicated, people who develop the proper sleeping habit will find it easy to fall asleep. The practice of cultivating a good sleeping habit is called *sleep hygiene*. While it may be difficult to cultivate this habit in the initial stages of this process, it will eventually be beneficial because it will improve your sleeping routine. While it can take some effort, perseverance, and planning, sleep hygiene will improve your overall sleep routine. The general principles of sleep hygiene include:

1. *Have a fixed time to go to sleep and wake up*

Once you have a set time to go to bed, you know you must be in bed at that particular time. For example, if your set time is 9 pm, once it's 9 pm, you know you have to leave everything you're doing and get in bed. Maintain this fixed time even when you're on vacation. Furthermore, going to bed at a set time will help your body adjust to a regular schedule that will ideally help your circadian rhythm be in line with a regular day cycle.

2. *Follow a daily and strict routine before bed*

Our realities are different, so it might be difficult to tell you a specific routine to follow. However, it's essential to go through the same routine every night. This routine will help train your brain, and once you start this process, your brain will ultimately know it's time to sleep.

3. *Limit daytime naps*

Daytime or evening napping can make it much harder to fall asleep when you need to at night.

4. *Create a room that makes you comfortable*

Let's focus on the interior of your bedroom. If, for example, your bed is uncomfortable, then you should consider changing it. Rearrange your room and make sure the sunlight is not facing your bed directly, or you may need to also get thicker window blinds or curtains to prevent excess light from coming in. Arrange the bedroom and make it the most comfortable place possible. You may also need to move the television out of your room if you have one. To get the right quality and quantity of sleep, it is important to do everything necessary to limit your sleep disruption.

5. *Limit the use of any technological device in your room*

Unfortunately, the light from your phone, tablet, or laptop can make it harder to fall asleep. Limit screen time leading up to your set bed time, and, more importantly, avoid using any devices in bed.

6. *Daily exercise*

Exercise is beneficial to your health and mood. To improve your sleep, you need to exercise more, and it doesn't have to be heavy exercise either — a light and regular exercise routine will do. Exercise, such as running, walking, or swimming can dramatically improve your health in a multitude of ways.

7. *Keep a sleep diary*

A sleep diary helps you track your progress and enables you to know what to focus on to better improve your sleep and mood. In a sleep journal, you can note your routine, bedtime, wake up time, and how you feel the next day. The sleep journal also helps give your counselor or doctor detailed information about your progress. This can be useful information to help them understand your sleep habits and problems.

In reality, there is no single best routine for sleep hygiene, therefore, it's fine to make some modifications to the list above based on your own needs and preferences.

Please remember that while the guide in this chapter is thorough and well-researched, it is not a replacement for advice from a medical doctor or counselor. Consult your primary health physician if you have any concerns about normal sleeping patterns, medical conditions, or treatments.

2.2 How our thoughts can negatively affect us

We all have an inner critic that challenges our every thought or action. At times, this little inner voice is needed to help us stay motivated toward reaching our goals. For example, our inner voice reminds us that what we're about to eat or drink contains many calories, or that it isn't good for us, or that the actions we're about to take aren't wise. However, this voice is often more harmful than helpful, especially when it becomes increasingly negative over time. We often find ourselves harboring unproductive thoughts that are harmful to our mental and physical health. In fact, we can think ourselves right into a problem, when really, there may not be a problem at all, or if there is, it isn't as difficult as we may think. It's very common to have unproductive thoughts, and unfortunately, we can carry them with us everywhere we go. Oftentimes, people will use the same unhealthy thinking pattern again and again throughout their lifetime. Unfortunately, most people are not even aware of how counterproductive this thinking pattern can be, so they end up thinking about the same thing over and over again, even if they know it isn't helpful.

"If you realize how powerful your thoughts are, you would never think of negative thoughts."

~ *Peace Pilgrim*

This process, when utilized in moderation, is known as the human self-talk process, and if left unmonitored/unchecked, it can become an obsession and ultimately have a negative impact on our physical and psychological health. Basically, negative thoughts or self-talk is an inner dialogue within you that may limit your ability to believe in yourself and ultimately can hinder you from reaching your full potential. In short, this is any thought that hinders you from becoming as productive as possible.

Overthinking can kill your happiness

We all experience negative thoughts from time to time, and further, they can cause significant stress to ourselves and everyone else around us. This inner critic or self-talk comes in many forms, and it must be controlled, so that it doesn't transform into a totally negative behavior. Mediating our inner critic may sound like critical parenting, a boss at work scolding us, or even a friend from the past advising us about some aspect of our lives. This process may even lead to cognitive distortion. Becoming aware of any unhelpful thoughts is the first step to making positive changes in your life. Read through the following examples of unhelpful thinking patterns and think about how they may affect you. Consider whether you've experienced any of these before, or if you are experiencing any at the moment, so that you can determine how best to change your thinking process. With the easy exercises in this chapter, you can focus on the cause of these thoughts, reframe your problems, and take back control of your thought processes.

Here's what you need to know about your thinking pattern and its effect on your body, mind, life, and loved ones.

How your thinking pattern impacts your mood, mental health, and life.

Types of unhelpful thoughts:

Labeling: This is when a person attaches a label to themselves due to past failure or events. For example, when a child says, "I'm a failure" because they failed a test at school, or when a teenage girl says, "I'm perfect" because she feels she is more beautiful than her friends.

Should/Must: These modal auxiliaries are used to indicate expectations. The use of these words about ourselves or others often creates high expectations. For example, a child can say, "I must become a millionaire by age 18," therefore, setting up the expectation that this should happen.

Catastrophe: This is a situation where a person thinks about a terrible situation. In fact, they think about the worst thing that can happen in every situation. This type of thought process makes them blow things out of proportion. For example, when a person with this type of thinking pattern loses their job, at that moment, they are already thinking about how that loss will also result in the loss of their house, wife, savings, etc.

All or nothing: This is also known as *black and white thinking*. People with this type of mindset place unnecessary expectations on themselves, and they don't compromise at all. It's either they achieve their set goal, or they abandon the entire goal altogether. Take, for example, a teenager seeking to gain admission into Oxford University, but then he doesn't end up getting accepted. On the other hand, he was lucky enough to gain admission to a lower-tier university. If the teenager has an "all or nothing" mentality, they will refuse to pursue their studies at the lower-tier university, and would, instead, continue trying to get accepted into the university of their choice, which is Oxford, in this case.

Mental filter: People with this thought process focus on what suits their own narrative, which often means a fraction of the evidence, while they ignore the *big picture*.

Naturally, the human brain filters tend to ignore the positives, while instead, noticing the negatives. In this way, we are more likely to notice or even ruminate on our failures and ultimately disregard our successes. For example, when a child comes home with their report card, it says they failed a subject, but that they also excelled in their remaining nine subjects. If their parent possesses the mental filter type of thought process, they are more likely to focus on the one subject that their child failed rather than focus on the other subjects where their child succeeded.

Mind reading: These people tend to occupy a place in another person's brain. In other words, they have an opinion about what the next person is thinking. For example, a mind reader may say," I know what she's thinking — I know she hates me."

You may more than likely be personally/intimately familiar with a few of the thinking patterns discussed above, and that's okay. What's more important, however, is to consider how often you tend to use any of these patterns, and how well those thinking patterns serve you in your everyday life.

Fortunately, there are methods and practices to help you turn your outlook around. These techniques take practice, but they don't work overnight.

In our case study, Mrs. Smith discovered she was in a rumination loop; she was dwelling on the fear of things that haven't happened. She was always thinking about the worst-case scenario, to the point where she could hardly think about anything else. In short, she was always worried about work, life, and family.

Some of us are like Mrs. Smith — we think about our problems, and although we need to think about our problems to an extent, we need to change our approach, if we're serious about solving them. We may find ourselves in a situation where we're stuck in a loop, and the same thought or thoughts are repeated again and again. We may even become anxious as a result of our thinking. It may even be killing us on the inside, but we don't know how to stop it. Mrs. Smith, on the other hand, was ready to escape this rumination loop, and here's how she did it:

How to prevent your thinking pattern from hurting you

There are many ways to prevent your thinking pattern from disrupting your mood and ultimately your daily life. However, it's important to note that different strategies work better for different people, so try a few of the techniques below and see which ones are most effective for you.

- **Catch Your Critic**

The first step towards changing your thinking pattern is to notice when you're self-critical, or when these thoughts are springing up, so you can stop them. For example, an ideal time for this would be if you start noticing that your inner voice is telling you things that are hurtful, such as things you wouldn't even say to your friends.

- **Thoughts and Feelings Aren't Always Reality**

Noticing and acknowledging your negative thoughts may seem like an obvious observation, but your thoughts and feelings are not always reliable. Therefore, you are not always accurate in your self-assessment — you can be either too hard or too soft on yourself. Which leaves the thoughts you have about yourself questionable and ultimately unreliable. Like everyone else, your thoughts can be skewed, subject to bias, and they can ultimately influence your mood.

- **Give Your Inner Critic a Nickname**

It's refreshing to give your inner critic a name. So, let's say you name your inner voice Coco. Once the inner voice comes up with a frivolous or negative idea, you could say

"Coco is doing her thing again." Naming your inner critic will help you separate your inner voice from your actual personality. Once you think of your inner critic as a force outside of yourself, by giving it a goofy nickname, it will become easy to realize you don't necessarily need to agree with all that it tells you. Once you realize this, your thoughts will become less threatening, and you will begin seeing them as a joke. You may even laugh about it and wonder how silly some of your ideas sound.

- **Change Negativity to Neutrality**

Negative thoughts flourish in your mind because you allow them to. When the negative talk starts, it can sometimes be challenging to force yourself to stop that train of thought in its track. However, you may be able to catch yourself by changing the intensity of the language of your thoughts. For example, "I hate having Kelvin around" may transform into, "I don't enjoy Kelvin's company." Or, "I'm stupid for acting that way," may become "I could have acted better." In short, when your self-talk includes more subtle language, it will prove to be less powerful and influential, and ultimately less *negative*.

- **Cross-Examine Your Inner Critic**

Our thoughts can cause considerable damage because they often go unchallenged. You may feel it's all in your head, and others don't know what you're thinking, so there's no need to challenge these thoughts in the first place. It's essential to put your ideas in check by filtering them and asking yourself how real your thoughts are. You'll be shocked to realize that a vast majority of your thoughts are exaggerated, and putting your thoughts in check can remove their damaging influence.

- **Think Like a Friend**

At its worst, your inner critic can sound like your enemy. Often, we say things to ourselves that we would never say to a friend. To reverse this process, when you catch yourself speaking negatively to yourself in your head, you can change this by imagining that you are saying those same things to a close friend. If you know that you wouldn't say those things to them, and you also know you wouldn't want a friend to speak to you in the same way either, then it's high time you stopped doing that to yourself. Talking to friends is a great way to shift your self-talk into a more positive experience, in general.

- **Shift Your Perspective**

Sometimes, we place a lot of emphasis on something by focusing on it for a long time. For example, you can make inquiries to know if what you're worried about will even matter in the short or long term. Another way to shift your perspective is to look at your problems from a greater distance. Just think of the world as a humongous place, and you're just a tiny part of it. This shift in perspective will remind you that most of your worries are not as significant as you make them seem. This method will also help you minimize your negativity, fear, and urgency in your negative self-talk.

- **Say It Aloud**

This method works like magic, so whenever you catch yourself thinking negative thoughts, merely saying them aloud can be of tremendous help. In other words, once you say them aloud, the thoughts can stop, knowing they are no longer confined to the space in your head. Talking to a friend about your ideas can often lead to a good laugh on how silly some of your ideas can be. Speaking to a friend about your thoughts is also therapeutic and can bring you much-needed support. Saying some of your negative self-talk around others can also remind you how unreasonable and unrealistic your thoughts sound. So, the physical act of saying these thoughts aloud will help you give your self-critic a break.

- **Stop That Thought**

Putting a stop to negative thoughts before they spiral out of control, can be a healthy habit to form. This is a practical method that is also known as *thought-stopping*. This method can take the actual form of snapping a rubber band on your wrist, so that you begin changing your thoughts as soon as a negative one enters your mind. You can also visualize a stop sign whenever a negative thought pops into your head. This practical method can help stop negative thoughts before they take up residence in your mind. Even more importantly, this method will help with repetitive or extremely critical thoughts like, *I'm stupid*, or, *I can't do that.*

- **Replace the Bad with Some Good**

This substitution method is one of the best routes to combating our negative self-critic because it allows us to replace negative thoughts with encouraging ones. It's as easy as replacing a bad habit with a good one. For example, you can substitute a bad habit of eating unhealthy food simply by eating healthy food. Just like replacing unhealthy food with healthy alternatives, you could also replace harmful thoughts with healthy, positive alternatives. Repeat this process until you feel you need to do less of it daily. It's a great way to develop a more positive way of thinking about yourself and life, in general.

Excessive rumination, negative self-talk, and engaging in self-criticism are all unhealthy thinking patterns. When this happens, you may find yourself in a situation where you're stuck in a loop, and the same thought or thoughts continue to repeat in your mind. However, you can change your thought process entirely by using the above methods.

2.3 Rivalry among colleagues at work

Competing with other people is an inherent part of our existence. The desire to be the best or at least better than others, especially our peers, can push us to work harder. It's interesting to note that competition among family members or peers isn't remotely unique to humans; all through their lifetime, animals also compete for survival. Therefore, rivalry among colleagues at work shouldn't come as a surprise. Regardless of the scale, forms, or the basis of a variety of things we do in the workplace, we are all in a competition. However, a problem can arise when we become consumed with the idea of becoming the best. We may let rivalry take over the innocent and straightforward desire to outdo the other person. When left unaddressed, rivalry between colleagues in the workplace can result in undue stress, anxiety, hatred, disgust, jealousy, anger, and troubled team dynamics. These negative emotions can set the stage for a much more serious conflict later. For instance, a minor spat in a multinational organization among the board members could lead to total drama and chaos. This type of drama is a sign of how dangerous an unchecked workplace rivalry can be.

"Peace is not the absence of conflict; it is the ability to handle conflict by peaceful means."

~Ronald Reagan

A rivalry between two colleagues can often be traced to insecurities, jealousy, hatred, anxiety, or disagreement. In fact, this rivalry might begin with a petty professional dispute. Still, it might quickly escalate into a competition about who should occupy the senior position in the organization, who earns the highest salary, who holds more responsibility, whose office is bigger or better, etc.

It's crucial to check workplace rivalry and tensions to prevent them from escalating to such dangerous levels that they disrupt the workplace. Below are the causes of workplace rivalry and tips to help you handle them.

Causes of rivalry among colleagues at work

Poor communication: Communication is an essential tool that helps humans coexist. The failure to communicate due to a difference in communication style can lead to rivalry at work. For instance, a manager assigned a job to each employee personally but refused to assign Mr. Smith's role directly to him. Instead, he told one of Mr. Smith's colleagues to communicate the assignment to

Mr. Smith. This attitude might make Mr. Smith feel offended and could even create animosity between the other colleagues and the manager. Poor communication at work can also cause employees to make false assumptions or start unsubstantiated rumors. Therefore, it's crucial to create and maintain the right kind of communication to avoid rivalry in the workplace.

Different temperaments among employees: In any organization, employees come from diverse locations with different experiences. Their experiences and upbringing will play a part in influencing their personality and outlook. When an employee fails to recognize and respect the diversity of their colleague's personalities, this will often lead to a constant misunderstanding, which may eventually lead to rivalry among them. For example, one of the employees may possess a direct and confrontational personality, where they speak their mind regardless of the outcome or consequences. An employee with this type of personality would offend an employee who is an introvert. The employee with the introverted personality may think the employee with the outspoken personality is rude, which may lead to hatred between them. Every organization is supposed to provide a platform that allows employees to embrace personality differences and inspire new employees to do the same. When every employee identifies and appreciates the other person's unique character traits, they will act more respectfully and maintain mutual respect in the workplace. A workplace environment that supports diversity will be non-judgmental and ultimately witness an increase in the expression of ideas and reduced workplace animosity.

"In business, when two people always agree, one of them is irrelevant."

~ William Wrigley

Different principles and value systems: Where there is a generational gap in the workplace, there can be an apparent difference in values and beliefs. The older employees may have a different value system from the younger employees. However, the difference in value or beliefs in and of itself is not the cause of rivalries in the workplace, but rather, the failure to accept the difference is. A misunderstanding may occur from opposing mood or thought processes and differences in communication styles. This friction may also be intensified by technological change. Regardless, every employee deserves to be heard, irrespective of their age, class, temperament, or occupation.

"Competition is a by-product of productive work, not its goal. A creative man is motivated by the desire to achieve, not by the desire to beat the other."

~ Ayn Rand

Competition in the workplace: In a situation where an employee's productivity is directly linked to their salary, there may be an intense rivalry between colleagues. Lately, more business organizations are promoting competition among their employees. This is healthy if it doesn't go beyond what is acceptable in the workplace, however, research has shown us that the reverse is often the case. An unhealthy competition at work can result in employee-to-employee abuse, to include insulting each other, which only harms communication in a pressure-packed environment. Every organization has to learn to use motivational methods or incentive packages, such as advancement, extra benefits, or an increase in salaries to inspire their employees to put their best into their work while also encouraging them to maintain a good relationship with one another.

How to stop rivalry among colleagues at work

Understand the source of resentment: First off, call a meeting to understand the cause of the rivalry or misunderstanding. The HR representative could ask all employees involved in the misunderstanding series of questions. Some of these questions could include: questions about each employee's performance, personality, views, beliefs, mood, temperament, etc. The HR representative could then delve deeper and reach the crux of the issue before it spirals into a negative, tense situation. The earlier the case is treated, the better.

Please refrain from taking pot-shots: It's very tempting to reply to a rude question with a well-rehearsed, rude answer in return. Giving an insecure colleague a taste of their own medicine in front of others, especially when you've resisted doing so for so long, could be very satisfying. But, for your own sake, it's advisable that you avoid this approach. Annoying your colleagues in this way will only bring you down to their level. It also pushes any potential resolution further away, leaving you vulnerable to their future verbal attacks, etc. Insecure people love to be the ones making all the attacks, and once you attack them in return, they feel offended. These types of people will always make sure you notice that they're ego is damaged. They will even try their best to get even at all costs. Therefore, when an insecure colleague tries to engage you in a verbal fight, try your best to refrain from responding, and simply walk away. It shows you're more mentally mature than they are. The best policy is not to provoke them at all.

Don't ask others to pick a side: Avoid office politics, and never choose a side when two individuals or groups of colleagues are fighting. Even more importantly, avoid putting yourself in an awkward situation where you'll have to pick a side to begin with. However, if you're already on a particular side, don't ask others to join you. And you should never put them in a position where they will have to join your team either. When you make or force employees to join a team, not only are you putting them in an awkward position, but this might get you into trouble with the HR team or the board of directors. Besides, involving others in your rivalry with a colleague only shows how scared and under-confident you are, even when the factors that led to the rivalry are in your favor.

Offer to resolve the tension: Take responsibility, even if you're right, or you were offended. Walk up to your colleague and offer to resolve the tension in order to establish peace, and, more importantly, for the sake of the company's growth. Look at it this way; regardless of the outcome, it's a win-win situation for you. If your colleague takes the peace offering, and the conflict is resolved, you'll be praised for taking the first step towards quashing the conflict. On the other hand, if your colleague rejects your offering, you'll still be commended for taking the necessary steps towards achieving a peaceful work environment.

Work hard: The best way to make your mark at work is to do the best you can in your particular role. Although drafting a comprehensive conflict resolution mechanism would be the ideal way to diffuse workplace rivalry, if you want to win the heart of the board and your fellow colleagues, then simply work hard to prove your merit. This is often the best way to win the heart of your critics and rivals.

Rivalry is rooted in our DNA. In other words, we are designed to fight for limited resources. People who work hard and achieve higher salaries, advanced skills, valuable knowledge, and better ideas will often be looked upon with envy and jealousy, which can eventually lead to rivalry with their colleagues. You'd be surprised to know that some people change their profession because of workplace rivalry. A healthy amount of rivalry is, in fact, necessary to improve productivity and individual efficiency. Still, the moment the competition becomes unhealthy to where it negatively affects productivity, an intervention will be required. As individuals, our best option at dealing with competition in the workplace is rising above it and making every effort to eliminate it, without focusing on who's right or who's wrong. It's impossible to please everyone you work with, and you are bound to offend one or two colleagues at some point, even if you don't intend to. Hence, don't fret over it, but, instead, use the tips above to resolve any rivalry at your workplace.

2.4 The unhealthy environment in the family and relationships

Our family and personal relationships, are the single most important influences in our lives. These relationships provide us with security, identity, and values for everyone involved. We learn about our sense of self and gain our basic understanding of the foundation of society from our family. This foundation includes family values, which provide us with our basic moral code. Therefore, an unhealthy family or relationship style can have a significant impact on our development and growth. Imagine the mental state of a child, brought up in an unhealthy environment where problems such as abuse, parent negligence, and alcoholism exist. These unhealthy behaviors by the parents or guardians will disturb the smooth functioning of the child and can lead to frequent arguments, fights, conflicts, and tension in the family. A family where neglect, conflict, and negative behaviors are constant is unhealthy and dysfunctional. Modern psychology classifies such families or relationships as those with *anxious systems*. A child or adult in an unhealthy family or relationship environment will experience a tremendous emotional disturbance, which will be evident in the child's behavior. Children from unhealthy homes will frequently exhibit behaviors such as:

◆ Excessive guilt
◆ Feeling responsible for others
◆ Anxiety
◆ Nervousness
◆ Being hard on themselves
◆ Poor communication skills
◆ Tense
◆ Anger
◆ Mood swings
◆ Low self-esteem

Basically, an unhealthy family or personal relationship is a situation where the normal healthy functioning of the family or relationship is disrupted by negative behaviors, such as neglect, abuse, apathy, and a lack of emotional support. This often means a situation where the relationship between each member of the family is tense and unnatural, and where the parents frequently abuse or neglect their children and other members of the family. The product of such families will often end up with low self-esteem, and they often grow up to raise their families in a similar, unhealthy manner. Thus, they will often continue the cycle of unhealthy personal and family relationships. On the other hand, a healthy family environment encourages support and encourages all family members to attain optimal growth while providing a safe space for emotional and physical growth.

> "In healthy families, we encourage our children to be loving and close to each other. In a narcissistic family, children are pitted against each other and taught competition."

> ~ Dr. Karyl McBride

Relationships in an unhealthy and dysfunctional family environment.

Ideally, everyone ought to grow up in an environment that makes them feel loved and ultimately valuable. People who grow up in a stable and healthy family environment are emotionally healthy and often have healthy relationships. However, people in an unhealthy family or personal relationship can find themselves in an unhealthy environment where their needs are curbed or frequently abused or criticized. In addition, there is mutual respect between family members in a healthy family environment, but in an unhealthy family environment, there is always tension and mistrust amongst family members. Also, the authority of the senior members of the family is often misguided. Besides, unhealthy families do not value apology and don't allow each family member's emotions to be expressed in a reasonable way.

In a family of six, living in one of the poorest areas in Brooklyn, an underemployed widow comes home to her young children. Strapped for cash as a single income household, all the children join her in offloading her bag. She had just gone to beg for leftover food at one of the restaurants down the street. Today is a lucky day because the restaurant chef was generous enough to add some baked beans to the macaroni that he gave them. They all join their mom as she prepares to serve the macaroni and baked beans for dinner. The mother is overworked, tired, and exhausted from begging for food, but she was left with no other choice. She constantly snaps at her children, too. In school, her children are always ridiculed because they wear the poorest quality clothes, shoes, and bags. Two of the eldest children, at some point, had thought of changing to a different school or stop going to school entirely. She eventually got engaged to one of the street traders on the street. Whenever the widow is not around, however, he often engages her daughters in a sexual way. The children reported the incident to their mom, but she would always ignore them because she believes they make up stories because they don't like the man. When she's angry, she frequently uses abusive language with the children and even goes as far as throwing objects at them.

Now, picture another scenario. One of the wealthiest families in California waits up all night for their 16-year-old daughter to get in. She left home in the early hours of the day and still hasn't returned. Both of the parents are worried. She appears drunk at the front door at two a.m., and a heated argument ensues, and her dad throws a lamp at her. The mom is helpless and confused; she doesn't know what to do, so she starts crying. The girl went to her room, packed all her belongings, and told her parent she was leaving their house. The father then locks the door to stop her from leaving, which, of course, leads to further heated arguments.

These are two examples of an unhealthy family environment, using two different settings, Brooklyn and California, and two different economic situations, the poor and the rich. An unhealthy family environment is not restricted to the poor or the rich; neither is it restricted to the economic background or a geographical location. Below are some of the factors responsible for an unhealthy family environment.

After witnessing an unhealthy environment in your own family and ultimately deciding those patterns will end with you and will not be passed down to the future generation, is an extremely brave and powerful decision.

- **Addiction**

When members of the family are addicted to drugs, gambling, or alcohol, they could care less about their duties and responsibilities to the family. For them, relationships, love, and family are a second priority, after their addiction. In terms of their preference, their addiction comes first before their family or any other relationship.

- **Violence**

Violent behavior from any member of the family, especially the mother or father, can break the family's foundation. The children or external family members may distance themselves from such a relationship because they don't want to live in fear of being physically and emotionally hurt. This type of distancing will lead to a lack of close interaction between the family members, which will only further damage the family unit.

- **Financial status**

The family unit's ability to provide financial support to sustain each family member is critical to the family's stability, as a whole. In a situation where one of the parents is dead, and the other is jobless or unemployed, as in the scenario above, there is often disunity and disorganization in the family.

- **Authority**

When the head of the family or relationship is controlling, as in the second scenario above, there is often a strong tendency to infringe on the rights of other members of the family and ultimately destroy their spouse or partner, and any semblance of a positive environment in the home, in an attempt to control each family member's activities.

- **Religion**

When a member of the family has a strong religious belief system, they might become rigid, thus forcing their beliefs on every member of the family, especially their children. Such desperate actions can limit freedom in the home, and the children or other family members may grow up to become hostile.

The circumstances that can lead to an unhealthy and dysfunctional environment within a family may vary. Besides, each situation may have a different impact on each family member or party involved in the relationship.

Characteristics of an Unhealthy and Dysfunctional Family Environment

An unhealthy family environment has unique characteristics, which often highlight the improper dynamics between members of the family. Here is what it feels like to have an unhealthy environment at home:

Poor communication: Family members in an unhealthy family environment often lack effective communication skills. Their inadequate skills can sometimes be the result of years of constant abuse. For example, in a situation where a child is trying to express themselves, and their parents tell them to "shut up," could lead to this level of poor communication. Oftentimes, members of the family will sweep the issue under the rug and simply move on without resolving the issue at all. A productive and encouraging environment or conflict resolution mechanism is simply missing. Instead, they can sometimes resort to shouting or throwing things at each other while in the middle of a misunderstanding.

Lack of empathy: Due to the lack of unconditional love between each family member, children, or other members of an unhealthy family may grow up to lack empathy. They may even try to be perfect in everything they do because failure, in any form, is subjected to behavioral correction, even when it is unnecessary. Members of the family may live in fear and are more than likely to be emotionally conditioned to hide their fears by becoming perfect in everything they do.

Prone to addiction: Children or other young members in a family often try to follow what the older members of their family are doing. So, once these children see their father or mother smoking, drinking, or abusing drugs, they often grow up to do the same, and sometimes, they battle with addiction because they need an extra support system to cope with life.

Mental issues: As a result of drug abuse, smoking, and drinking, children from an unhealthy family environment may have a higher rate of developing mental health issues at an early age. They also experience a stronger likelihood of suffering from genetic illnesses due to their parent(s) drug abuse.

Controlling behavior: In a situation where the oldest members of the family are religious fanatics, they often focus on controlling every aspect of a family member's social, religious, and emotional life. This could stunt their family member's ability to grow and also, as a result, end up encouraging rebellious behavior. This level of control only creates self-doubt in the children in the home, and they often grow up to have serious trust issues.

Perfectionism: As stated earlier, the children who come from an unhealthy family environment try their best to achieve perfection in everything they do because their parents always put excessive pressure on them to achieve perfection. Sometimes, parents may go as far as emotionally blackmailing these family members to make them achieve the parent's desired results. The fear of failure combined with the physical and emotional consequences that naturally come with failure, can trigger these children or family members to grow up to become perfectionists.

Criticism: Family members who come from an unhealthy home life were likely criticized often for their lack of physical or mental prowess, or even for their behavior, in general. In other words, the only means of correction in an unhealthy home is criticism. These family members often grow up to doubt their every move. In turn, they constantly seek validation from other people at the expense of their own happiness, values, and self-worth.

Lack of privacy: Family members from an unhealthy family environment can often lack privacy boundaries because their parents or guardians constantly invaded their privacy from the beginning. In a family environment like this, the adults feel the need to constantly check up on each family member, so that they know what they are doing. Sometimes they go as far as deciding which university the child will attend or which partner the child will date, so that they can keep a constant eye (and ultimately, control) on the child.

Violence and abuse: Physical abuse is common in a toxic family environment, as we witnessed in the scenario above where the father throws a lamp at his daughter because he's angry. Members of this type of family may experience a strong degree of verbal, sexual, physical, and emotional abuse. It's even more devastating to know that these individuals will often adopt the mindset that the physical, mental, and emotional abuse they experienced while growing up is normal.

How to overcome the negative effects of an unhealthy family environment.

At a glance, overcoming the challenges of an unhealthy family environment may seem difficult or even impossible. But with perseverance and patience, it is, in fact, possible. However, you need to first acknowledge the various emotional and physical challenges that you had witnessed when you lived in an unhealthy environment and then follow the steps below to make any necessary changes in your life.

If you are a product of an unhealthy family life, make sure a healthy family comes from you.

1. **Take responsibility**

It's pretty difficult to make a drastic, life-changing decision without also taking responsibility for it. As a victim of an unhealthy personal relationship or family life, you ultimately have the choice to remain a victim of your past circumstances, *or* you have the choice to overcome the cards you were dealt, so that you can work towards becoming a healthy individual who is emotionally and physically stable. Of course, you can't change the past, but you can change both the present and the future by taking responsibility for your physical health and mental well-being. Consider going to therapy if you feel you need it, and speak with your doctor about your experiences if it will help you feel better. It is important to do everything in your power to overcome every trait of an unhealthy family environment.

2. **Seek help**

As stated in the first point above, it's important to seek professional help, especially in severe cases. It can be very difficult to deal with low self-esteem on your own. Therefore, you need the support of a medical professional. It's also advisable to open up to your spouse or friend, and let them know what you're going through and how much you need their support and love.

3. **Be creative**

One of the best ways to deal with emotions or how you feel, in general, is to channel your feelings into a creative outlet. This will help you express yourself better and in a more comprehensive manner. For example, you could write, keep a journal, draw, paint, or act. More importantly, make sure those negative feelings don't get the best of you. Channel them into your creative work. Not only will this make you more productive, but it will also help you gain better control of your emotions.

4. **Trust people around you**

When you've experienced years of abuse and distrust, it can be very difficult to trust people or let strangers into your life. However, we still need to trust someone, or at least have someone we can talk to when our hearts are heavy, or even someone we can cry to, and ultimately, someone we can trust. In summary, it's important to trust someone in your life. Knowing that you have someone you can trust isn't only reassuring, but it's also therapeutic.

5. **Forgive**

Forgiveness is the first step in the healing process. It's hard to fully let go of the unhealthy thoughts or pain of your past while you're still holding on it. Your parents or guardian may have harassed or abused you due to their ignorance of what was right or wrong at that particular time in your life. However, you could seek justice in a court of law if you feel that getting justice would also make you feel better or ultimately help you heal. Forgiveness is therapeutic; it can give you the comfort of starting from a clean slate (tabula rasa), embrace forgiveness, and experience freedom from the mental prison of an unhealthy family environment.

An unhealthy family environment will often lead to a dysfunctional family that is emotionally unstable, and therefore affecting every member of the family, especially the children. If you want to be free from the mental torture of an unhealthy family environment, take responsibility, and make the first move. There is a lot of help available to you, and always speak with your primary health physician if you have further questions.

2.5 Bad habits

Habits are behaviors that help us thrive and live with ease. Our habits help us adapt as well. Also, depending on which habits we adopt, they can also lead to us looking our best or even in becoming experts in our field. Just like robots, our habits control us, and in some ways, help define our personality. However, it's very difficult to change our habits, and it's even more difficult to change *bad habits*. Once a habit is programmed into our bodies, it can be very hard to change it. Of course, not all habits are created equal because a habit can either be good or bad. For instance, a bad habit can involuntarily work against us, while a good habit can develop, uplift, strengthen, and even nurture us. Although bad habits don't uplift or help us progress, we realize that people are more aware of (and worried about) their bad habits, without taking the time to notice or praise themselves for their good habits.

"One bad habit often spoils a dozen of good ones."

~Napoleon Hill

It's important to note that not all bad habits are necessarily physical or conspicuous. Habits such as swearing, picking your nose, smoking, biting your fingernails, consuming excessive quantities of alcohol, overeating, and consuming junk food are all examples of *bad physical* habits. In contrast, *bad* habits, such as hatred, backstabbing, gossiping, harboring resentment, or even an unstable mood, can be regarded as *innate* or *semi-visible* bad habits. This type of bad habit, although not seen, is more psychological in nature. These hidden bad habits are meant to perpetuate mental and emotional negative effects on a victim, which can, of course, be very detrimental. All bad habits have the psychological and physical capability to damage or ruin the life of the individual who harbors them. We ought to be conscious of these habits and make a firm resolution to transform them into good habits.

> "A bad habit cannot be tossed out of the window; it must be coaxed down the stairs one step at a time."
>
> ~ *Mark Twain*

Effect of bad habits on our emotions

It's nine a.m. on a Tuesday, and retired Capt. Kelvin is on his boat with a bottle of whiskey in his right hand and a cigarette in the other. Neighbors are furious and worried about the retired captain's reckless lifestyle, but he seems less worried about the rumors going around town about him. The captain seems more occupied with is drinking and smoking. He's seated on the deck of his speed boat, but then, the negative self-talk creeps in. The captain starts talking negatively to himself. "I'm too old to achieve anything worthwhile. All I have left are my cigarettes and whiskey. Why are these thoughts always disturbing me?" he asked himself. He also thought about his wife, and said, "I haven't forgiven her; she left with half of my wealth, and now she's with Donald. Donald! Donald, the fisherman. Can you imagine? She left me for a fisherman. She's so stupid." After a while, he fell asleep. Two weeks later, the neighbors of the retired captain received news of his demise. The doctor had informed them that one of the captain's lungs was severely damaged, which made him vulnerable to the flu. In other words, the captain died earlier than expected due to his reckless lifestyle choices and habits.

Habits Harm your Emotional Health: Negative self-talk capitalizes on an individual's misery. Consider the story of retired Captain Kelvin; the negative self-talk seemed to creep in while he was engaging in bad habits (i.e., drinking and smoking). In other words, his bad habits created a conducive environment for his negative self-talk to flourish. You witnessed him going on about how old he had become, and that he could no longer achieve anything in life even before his smoking habit damaged his lungs (a bad habit, which sadly made him vulnerable to the flu and eventually killed him). When you provide the platform for negative self-talk and habits to blossom, they will cripple your emotional and physical health and make you feel doubtful about everyone and everything. This type of mindset will attract even more negative and harmful circumstances that will only continue to reinforce the doubt and paranoia you are feeling. In the end, this will only make you paralyzed in most if not all areas of your life. Negative self-talk and bad habits are unhealthy, unhelpful, and very limiting. Do not let your mind be invaded by negative self-talk, and remember there's always greater power in positive self-talk than in negative self-talk.

Overthinking: Negative self-talk can lead to overthinking and ultimately cause sleepless nights, complicated health issues, and even deteriorating health. Overthinking occupies the mind with excessive worry and anxiety. It makes you think over a situation repeatedly, yet it does not offer any productive solutions. It's okay to be worried about some issues, but rather than letting the negative self-talk take control, work towards achieving a practical solution. When you feel you can't solve the problem, it is okay to let such a situation go or put it on hold in the meantime. Rest your brain and mind by getting more sleep. A rested brain and mind will produce more proactive thoughts than an exhausted one. Helpful and practical ways to overcome overthinking, fear, and anxiety include: praying, exercising, meditating, dancing, writing, painting, and doing yoga.

Holding emotional grudges: In the earlier scenario, you could see that retired Captain Kelvin still had an emotional grudge against his ex-wife. He said he wouldn't forgive her because, according to him, she took half of his wealth, and she's now with Donald. Holding an emotional grudge is a product of bad behavior, and it will continue to affect your mood and mental state until you let go and forgive your offender(s). It wouldn't be all that surprising to know smoking, drinking, and failing to forgive his ex-wife led Captain Kelvin into smoking and drinking in the first place. Learn from his story. In short, he is now dead, while his ex-wife is probably having the time of her life with Donald, the fisherman. Captain Kelvin's refusal to let go led him deeper into his bad habits, and, as a result, he lost his life. Learn to let go of things that are beyond your power and control. Always live in the present.

Mental habits and mood/emotion management.

1. Withdraw and understand what triggers your emotions

External forces often trigger our emotions. For example, a bad habit or emotion is often a reaction to something disturbing. Try to identify what it is, and make sure you find a way to avoid it. This *choice* will help you lead an anger-free life. Of course, this method isn't only applicable to anger, so it can be used in the face of all other negative emotions and bad habits. The best way to deal with these emotions and bad habits is to avoid them as much as you can.

2. Cultivate a positive mindset

Positivity is contagious; when you make an attempt to think and speak positively, it can be difficult for negative self-talk to interfere. Talking, thinking, and acting in a positive way can create a positive environment. When you're angry or upset about anything, think about the silver lining. There's always something good in everything. Train yourself to see the good in everyone and every situation, so that you become mentally stronger.

3. Limit negativity

This means limiting (or better yet, eliminating) anything negative about yourself. Whether it's your eating or drinking habits, if they are negative, you must limit them. Limit your negative thoughts in addition to any negative friends around you.

4. Don't react immediately to every argument

Arguments and misunderstandings will always happen. However, when they do, it's important to react to them conservatively. If, however, you respond immediately, things could escalate quickly, but when you take your time before you respond, you will be calmer and ultimately be in a better position to find a resolution.

Section No. 3. Awareness of emotions is the first step toward controlling them.

3.1 Anger and its negative effects

> "Anger doesn't solve anything. It builds nothing, but
> it can destroy everything."
>
> *~Thomas S. Monson*

University of Kansas football player Anthony Ray Williams, also known as *Pooka Williams*, has a reputation for being a "hothead." On December 6, 2018, he was arrested and charged with domestic battery, which led to his suspension from all team activities, pending investigation. This infraction could lead to a huge fine or jail time, and in the worst-case scenario, it could cost him his promising career. It is impossible to know what prompted Pooka Williams to lash out in this situation without getting into his head or at least trying to see things from his point of view. However, if he is like every other person suffering with anger, he may find it difficult to actually control his anger because he may not even understand the root cause of it.

"If you are patient in one moment of anger, you'll escape a hundred days of sorrow."

~Chinese Proverb

Like all other emotions, anger is a normal one that we all experience from time to time. Anger serves a purpose, too; it notifies us that we are suffering from some form of distress. Although anger can be uncomfortable both mentally and physically, it still helps us address our underlying needs or perceived threats. Usually, anger can be a reaction to subtle, uncomfortable feelings, such as disappointment, sadness, hurt, anxiety, embarrassment, or shame. However, these feelings or emotions may not be acknowledged. Even more, unprocessed anger, or the inability to control our anger, can lead to conflict, problems at work, depression, substance abuse, social isolation, and even incarceration. These and many other adverse effects are the consequences of unprocessed anger.

The anatomy of anger.

People express their anger in many different ways. Some people like Pooka Williams, physically express it by being aggressive or by punching another person. While others express their anger by directing at themselves. This is known as *passive-aggressive anger*. Some people also deny their anger and can become silent or withdrawn. None of the listed options is a healthy reaction to anger. Due to our biological makeup, or even how we were treated while growing up or with family members later in life, we may not have learned other ways to manage our anger. Anger usually begins with an event or a series of events that trigger your internal harmony and well-being. These events could be the result of another person's negative behavior towards you or some of other circumstances. It could also be the result of a series of negative imaginary situations or events that combined to affect your mood.

Anger is one letter short of danger.

Regardless of the cause of the anger, how you respond is a product of a series of your expectations about how you feel people should behave in a particular situation or about how life should play out. Some of these expectations often happen to be unrealistic. For example, you may feel your spouse should always be emotionally available when you need them, which may not work for them. Or, you may feel that water is a basic necessity, and therefore, you shouldn't pay to have clean water. When you have these expectations, then experiencing the unavailability of your spouse or getting the weekly/monthly water bill may trigger you to respond in anger.

Anger could also be the result of how you choose to view and assess a triggering event. For example, you may think an event means something that it actually doesn't, such as when your boyfriend or girlfriend comes home late due to their workload at the office, and you interpret that to mean they are cheating on you. In such a situation, being more aware of your thought processes can help you avoid an unnecessary fight.

Healthy ways to manage anger.

One of the healthiest ways to manage anger and prevent it from becoming physically or emotionally destructive involves self-reflection. The use of self-reflection as a tool in anger management further consists of the use of one of the sub-categories of self-reflection, which include: mindfulness, meditation, self-compassion, and self-awareness.

Mindfulness and Meditation: Practicing mindfulness and meditation will help you observe your emotions without reacting to them or becoming overwhelmed with the possibility of you acting out of control. This practice creates an awareness that allows you to think about the choices available to you in response to anger. Besides, this practice also teaches you that your emotions or physical reactions are only temporary, and they are never permanent. Mindfulness gives you the time necessary and more freedom to react in the best way possible in every situation. For example, through mindfulness, when you're angry, you can tell yourself, "This is a feeling I am experiencing right now. It will pass." This thinking process will make you more mindful and, ultimately, more in control. This awareness also helps you accept your thoughts and feelings. Therefore, you don't have to push them away, but instead, you'll learn to embrace your emotions and experiences while you continue to work on yourself to become more mindful of them.

"You've been criticizing yourself for years, and it hasn't worked. Try approving of yourself and see what happens."

~ *Louise Hay*

Self-compassion: Once you're mindfully aware of your emotions, self-compassion is the second phase. Self-compassion helps you become sensitive, kind, understanding, and accepting towards yourself without being negative. It is the conscious effort to offer kindness and understanding to yourself when you're going through difficult times. It is about seeing yourself as a human who isn't perfect, but, rather, as one who's willing to work through the process necessary to achieve all-around growth. It is about valuing yourself as someone worthy of everything, including love and respect. It embodies neither self-pity nor self-indulgence, but rather a healthy affirmation of yourself. The practice of self-compassion allows you to judge your emotions less harshly, and it also helps you recognize anger as a sign of underlying pain that must be addressed. When self-compassion and mindfulness skills are practiced together, they promote emotional sensitivity, enhance the understanding of the source of the emotion, and provides a guideline for safe and effective communication.

"Self-awareness is a key to self-mastery."

~ *Gretchen Rubin*

Self-awareness is the act of being aware of who you are. It is an act of psychological evaluation in an attempt to understand why you talk, act, or think the way that you do. It is an act of soul-searching and self-discovery that may go as far back as when you were still a child. Self-awareness skills can help you look at your experience and further your capacity experience anger in a healthy way. Self-awareness is critical because it enables you to understand who you are. It's easy to get lost, and it's also easy for people to label you with a personality based on your actions and reactions. However, that isn't who you are. Going through the process of self-awareness will help you uncover a lot of secrets about yourself and ultimately help you become mentally, physically, and psychologically balanced. By reflecting on your thoughts and being open to new ways of thinking and understanding your personal experiences and emotions, you can learn how to be more compassionate towards yourself and others.

Your commitment to managing your anger would be beneficial to you and everyone around you. In addition to learning how to manage our anger, mindfulness, self-compassion, and self-awareness are necessary for personal growth. They can lead you towards a positive relationship by making you more compassionate of the people around you. It may take a lot of discipline and courage to control your anger, and there may be setbacks along the way, however, while you can choose to be compassionate towards yourself and others at any point, you will have to continually build your self-awareness in order to manage your anger effectively. But, eventually, understanding and managing your anger will lead to a happier, positive life that may save your career and personal relationships.

3.2 Negative thinking and it how can be limited

> "Train your mind to see the good in everything. Positivity is a choice. The happiness of your life depends on your thoughts."
>
> *~Marc and Angel*

I know a retired nurse, who is a full-time resident of the *negative thinking zone*, or, rather, she has a case of *Eeyore syndrome*. She saved money for years to go to Hawaii on a dream vacation. This trip meant everything to her, and she could die afterward knowing she fulfilled her life-long dream of visiting the islands. However, once she finally arrived, it rained constantly, and her vacation was ruined.

I'll be giving you the full details of our interaction to help you understand the adverse effect of residing in the negative thinking zone, and why you need to take proactive steps to stop doing it.

We met during a political rally in Florida. We both realized we share the same political values and beliefs, and then our conversations became more interesting when I realized she was from North Carolina. She told me about her projects, and I was interested. I told her I would love to partner with her because I have always been passionate about what she's currently working on. After the rally, we exchanged contact information so we could remain in touch, however, during several of our conversations, I realized that she was a full-time resident of the negative thinking zone and, therefore, suffering from Eeyore syndrome because she was never happy or excited about our progress, nor does she see the good in most things.

Experiencing a negative thought changes your whole perspective of thinking.

Let's just say, this woman could win a $1 million lottery jackpot, and when people are about to congratulate her, her attitude would be, "It's horrible that the government is against me. They're requesting that I pay federal and state taxes on the jackpot, so now they're planning to take over $20,000, and I'll only wind up with only $980,000. Why do bad things always happen to me?" She's the type of person you want to smack on the head and shout, "SNAP OUT OF IT!"

When she returned from her vacation, she wasted no time telling me everything that went wrong, how it rained non-stop, how the hotel staff was rude to her, and how the cellular network was terrible. But she failed to tell me things that went right. So, the ranting when on and on. I made her feel comfortable and let her just vent. "Oh my God," she said, exasperated. "Do you know how long I've saved for this vacation? I feel wasted right now. I should have realized something like this would happen. My sister and her husband went to Hawaii last year, and they had a great time! My boss and his wife just got back two weeks ago from their vacation, and everything was so nice. But, no, not for me! The weather was horrible from the day I arrived. I shouldn't have even gone on that trip. The rain ruined everything! Are you there...? Hello..." It's been that way ever since I met her. Why would I expect anything else?

Let's face the facts. The fact remains that the rain in Hawaii didn't ruin her dream vacation. What actually destroyed it was her constant failure to see anything good in an otherwise bad situation. Her inability to see the silver lining in the dark cloud ruined her vacation. It was her thoughts about the bad weather that reinforced her pre-existing negative emotions that ultimately ruined her vacation. Of course, it would be nice if the weather was on her side during the trip, but because her focus and energy were on what wasn't working, she didn't give herself the chance to have a good time. It is practically impossible to have a successful result if your negative thoughts are more frequent than your positive ones. When you allow your current circumstance to determine your emotions, your peaceful state deteriorates. In this process, your happiness is replaced with other negative emotions, such as anger, disgust, and sadness. That's how you get a bad case of Eeyore Syndrome.

She allowed herself to create a thinking pattern that was causing a negative emotional response, and that ended up setting off an unhealthy physical response. You don't need to be a doctor to know that during her confrontation with one of the hotel staff members in Hawaii, her heart was racing, her stomach was tight, and she simply wasn't feeling right. These are the psychological side effects of negative emotions. She has created a deep and dreadful cycle for herself by continually meditating on her negative emotions and thought processes. It's even worse to know she will continue to relive the entire ordeal of her experience in Hawaii each time she tells the story. This will further exasperate her negativity, which is more commonly understood as *the snowball effect*.

Why can't I get a break?

Why does this always happen to me?

My life really sucks.

The world is against me.

I'm sure it wouldn't have worked anyway.

Why are they unnecessarily happy?

I shouldn't have gone to see him/her today.

These are typical examples of the thought processes of someone suffering from Eeyore syndrome.

Residing in the negative thinking zone means that regardless of the silver lining of a situation, or whatever good that may come your way, you will constantly pay more attention to the negative part. That is, you will always find something wrong with every good thing. The negative thought process, in this case, is a reflection of your lack of confidence and trust in normal life events. Furthermore, this makes you see yourself as a victim, and your appreciation of anything good life has to offer ultimately becomes distorted. However, our thought process isn't created, much less developed, in a day; it is something we unconsciously develop and, therefore, can proactively change. Instead of focusing and whining about a negative situation, make an attempt to see something positive in the situation. After all, the situation could be much worse than you imagined. Be grateful for a little light in the darkness. Choose to be a victor rather than a victim. That is the only methodological way to shift your thought process from negative to positive. Of course, it will be a gradual process, but I believe that you will pull through because you deserve all the happiness life has to offer. Let me walk you through, and together we can pull you out of the vicious cycle of negativity.

Causes of Negative Thinking?

Negative thinking is often a product of insecurity. However, it can be a result of other complex factors, such as illness, substance abuse, personality problems, and life experiences.

Negativity, like many things in life, can gradually become a habit. Constant criticism, subconscious negative thoughts, and denial can condition the brain to actually embrace sadness. When these negative tendencies control the more significant part of our thought processes, the brain is forced to distort the truth. This psychological change makes it even more difficult to break the negative thought cycle. However, the good news is that medical experts have confirmed that most habits can be broken in 21 days.

How Does Negativity Affect the Body?

As stated earlier, negative thinking or negative emotions are the body's natural response to threats, disasters, or heartache. In response to a perceived threat or stress, the human body is conditioned to deal with such situations by releasing cortisol into the bloodstream. The release of the cortisol makes you more alert and focused. However, high levels over a long period of time will often lead to severe health issues, such as poor digestion, while, at the same time, decreasing the immune system's ability to fight inflammation. That is why most health experts claim that negative people are ten times more likely to become sick than positive people.

Below are some of the harmful medical conditions associated with negative thinkers:

◆ Chest pain
◆ Social withdrawal
◆ Anxiety
◆ Fatigue
◆ Upset stomach
◆ Headache
◆ Sleep problems
◆ Depression
◆ Drastic changes in metabolism (over-eating or under-eating)
◆ Smoking or substance abuse as a way of coping

Overcoming Negativity

Our emotions create a pathway in our brains. Just as a negative thinking process develops over time, we can also reinforce positive self-talk and make positive thinking a habit. As I told my friend, "Happiness and positivity are a product of choice and not a product of circumstance." To overcome negative emotions, please follow the steps below:

Recognize what is real: The world isn't perfect, so there would never be a time where everything around you would be ideal. Therefore, to change your thinking patterns, you must learn to recognize what is real and embrace the fact that everything can't be perfect. This understanding will help you appreciate the positivity in the face of negativity.

Keep a journal: You might want to do what my friend did during her therapy stages; she started a *thoughts journal.* This helped her recognize her thinking patterns. She was able to observe her own positive and negative thoughts. For example, she was able to combat a reoccurring negative view with positive self-talk. Besides, the journal is a detailed account of your emotion and could be a helpful tool that your psychologist or counselor would work with.

Live in the moment: It's very difficult to stop being negative if you don't let go of past mistakes or the fear you may have about the future. You have to learn to counter every negative thought with a positive response. That's the only way to take control of your mind and thought processes.

Be positive: Try to become optimistic about every situation. Regardless of bad news or a series of events, try to be grateful for the little things that actually went right. When you consciously try to think positively, you leave little or no room for negative thoughts. Cultivate positive habits, such as spending time with loved ones or engaging in a group conversation. These habits will limit your reflection on negative things.

Channel your negativity into solutions: To be realistic, it's humanly impossible not to experience negative or unproductive thoughts, and we all have them occasionally. However, instead of whining and complaining, the negative thoughts should challenge positive thinkers to come up with a solution. For example, if a positive thinker realizes they are gaining more weight over the holiday, instead of complaining about the government's failure to make legislation that promotes eating healthy food, they could use that negativity/weight gain as fuel to start working out and living a healthier lifestyle.

Spend more time with positive people: when you spend a lot of time with a sadist, you may gradually become one. The same principle works when you spend time with an optimist. Negativity and optimism are both equally contagious. Therefore, spending quality time with optimistic people will help significantly in overcoming negativity.

It is humanly impossible to eradicate negative thinking. However, it can be reduced, and its psychological effect on us can be made irrelevant using the steps discussed above.

3.3 Explosive Anger

When Mark was 16 years old, he got in an argument with his younger brother at the park, resulting in his chasing his brother with a stick in his hand. At 21, after a messy breakup with his girlfriend, he went into her car, and he drove it into the garage door, damaging the vehicle and the building. At 27, his father confronted him to account for how he spent the money he made from the family real estate business. This caused him to fly into a rage and threaten his father's life.

"Anger is a bad advisor."

~Czech proverb

"I have always been a difficult child; as a kid, I got away with terrible and punishable behavior. Everyone, including me, just thought I was hotheaded, and, with time, maturity would make this negative behavior go away. I was wrong, however, because it never did, and as the years passed, I became even more violent," says Mark, now 32 years old. He disclosed that he ended up seeking psychiatric help months after the family took the business from him, and he went broke. "Somehow, I knew my behavior wasn't normal," muses Mark. "I guess, when I reflect on how my behavior has cost me several relationships, and it got to a point my parents wanted nothing to do with me, I knew I needed help."

Janet, 16, is described by her stepmother, Diane, as having a "strange personality." "When she's calm, she is an adorable, loving, and affectionate girl," says Diane, "however, when she's angry, she can become frightening and horrible. I don't understand this side of her." Janet, who splits her time between her parents' homes, has exhibited aggressive and violent behavior with her stepmother when she doesn't get what she wants. Diane had to call the police for assistance on two separate occasions during her visits. But Janet's father, Sam, a local trader, and the school Janet attends, have not witnessed her exhibit any aggressive or violent behavior. Her teachers admit she sometimes becomes angry, but her anger is normal and not more than what is expressed by other kids in her class.

Mark and Janet have been diagnosed with intermittent explosive disorder (IED) and are both undergoing treatment under the care of a mental health professional.

Everybody gets angry once in a while. However, when the degree of anger or aggression is out of proportion with the situation, it's a sign of a more complex psychological issue. Intermittent explosive disorder is a negative condition and chronic disorder that involves repeated, sudden impulsive, violent, and aggressive behavior or an angry outburst, where your reaction is out of proportion to the situation. This behavior manifests through aggressive and violent behavior such as road rage, throwing or breaking objects, domestic abuse, or any other form of tantrum. Intermittent explosive disorder begins from childhood and can continue into adulthood. The disorder's symptoms may decrease with age, but it will not go away, except when the patient is treated with medication, therapy, or both.

Symptoms

Intermittent explosive disorder (IED) can happen suddenly. This is the case when a person occasionally flares up without warning, and the episode usually lasts less than thirty minutes. IED can be chronic; in this case, a person can feel irritable, mad, aggressive, and chronically angry most of the time, or they can be separated by weeks of nonaggression. Symptoms of explosive anger and IED include:

◆ Irritability

- ◆ Rage
- ◆ Palpitations
- ◆ Physical violence
- ◆ Verbal tirades
- ◆ Chest tightness
- ◆ Racing thoughts
- ◆ Slapping, and pushing
- ◆ Increased energy
- ◆ Shouting matches

Unrestrained explosive anger can cause significant damage to you and your family and can cause negative consequences in the important aspects of your life, as it did for Mark. Hence, there is a need to prevent it. How do you prevent explosive anger?

Prevention

"The greatest remedy to anger is delay."

~ Lucius Annaeus Seneca

The treatment for IED is likely beyond your control. This disorder can only be treated through medication or therapy. However, these suggestions, in combination with treatment, can help you prevent explosive anger.

Practice relaxation techniques: Relaxation techniques, such as a deep breathing, yoga, and meditation may help you stay calm.

Cognitive restructuring: This is the practice of changing the way you think and react to situations using logic, rational thinking, and reasonable expectations to help you see and respond to situations in a more effective way. Practicing the methods you were taught in therapy can help you identify what triggers your anger and the best ways to respond to it.

Learn to improve your communication: Try to improve how you communicate with others. It is essential to listen to what comes up in your mind first, analyze and think about the best response, and then act upon it. Don't simply act, and then think afterward. The act of analyzing your actions in your head before acting will help you communicate with others more effectively.

Use problem-solving techniques: Work with your professional healthcare worker to develop a flexible and suitable problem-solving technique that can help you escape a situation that triggers your emotions. You could walk away, pray, refuse to reply, listen to music to calm down, or call a trusted friend to help calm you down. Anything would be excellent as long as it works for you.

Change your environment: Your environment may be filled with negative or unfriendly energy that makes you angry all the time. If this is the case, you may need to move to a more positive, encouraging environment.

Avoid alcohol and illegal drugs: These substances will increase the likelihood of your aggression and also damage your health.

Improve self-care: General well-being is as important as mental health, and it's also important to know they are intertwined. Therefore, what affects one affects the other. Getting good and consistent rest, exercising, and practicing proper stress management can increase your tolerance in the face of frustration.

Stick to your treatment: To prevent aggressive and explosive anger, it is vital to attend all of your therapy sessions, practice your recommended coping techniques, and if you are on medication, make sure you don't miss any doses, so that you avoid explosive episodes in the future.

Unfortunately, most people are like Mark; they don't even know they are suffering from a severe negative emotion known as explosive anger or IED until it destroys all they have worked for, and all that they care about. Take steps to protect yourself and your loved ones by applying the suggestions above in combination with your treatment therapy to stop these negative emotions from destroying your life.

Section No. 4. Ways to solve the problem

4.1 Improving self-esteem & self-confidence

> "I had to grow to love my body. I did not have a good self-confidence at first. Finally, it occurred to me I'm either going to love me or hate me. And I choose to love myself and everything kind of sprung from there. Things I thought weren't attractive became sexy. Confidence makes you sexy."
>
> ~Queen Latifah

Your sense of self-worth will influence every area of your life. Your relationships, job, in addition to your mental and physical health are a reflection of your self-confidence. But what helps you create a perception about yourself and your own abilities? The truth is that your level of self-esteem and confidence may have declined or increased due to the treatment you got from people in the past or simply from your own assessment of any given circumstance. When I started my business, one of the things that stopped me from going after my business goals was the fear of failure. Failure is a negative emotion that comes as a result of fear of the unknown, and because I was naive and lacked self-confidence, I short-changed myself. To some degree, we all face these negative emotions. Over the years, I have proactively read and conducted research on how to improve my self-esteem and self-confidence, and this has helped me overcome my fears and pursue my dreams. Undoubtedly, I still get scared, especially when the challenges ahead of me are overwhelming. Now, I have the right mindset and knowledge on how to improve my self-esteem and self-confidence, so I'm less scared than I used to be. I know I can beat fear and failure, and that I can break through the walls of negative emotions and come out on the other side as a victor.

It is nearly impossible to achieve your goals and break away from the stigmatization of failure if you have issues with low self-esteem and self-confidence. I know some writers will make a rigid distinction between self-esteem and self-confidence, which is good. In this chapter, I will be using self-esteem and self-confidence interchangeably for the sake of emphasis and to effectively drive home my points. However, there is a slight difference between these two psychological concepts. The difference is that low self-esteem is a mental battle, which makes you doubt if you're worthy of respect and love from others, while a lack of self-confidence is a mental struggle to believe in your own abilities. But, in the end, the decrease in self-esteem or the lack of self-confidence can create or leads to negative emotions.

This chapter was inspired by a friend, Nick from Finland, whose sense of self-worth and self-confidence seems to be declining, and he needs help on how to strengthen them.

Causes of low self-esteem and a lack of self-confidence?

Usually, factors that affect our self-esteem and self-confidence vary. Your confidence may change overnight, or the change may be a gradual process that might make it even more challenging to recognize. However, two clear factors responsible for a decline in self-esteem and the lack of self-confidence are fear and failure, which are classified under the sub-categorization of negative emotions. Life experiences, such as the ones listed below could be responsible for low self-esteem and a lack of self-confidence:

◆ Discrimination or stigmatization
◆ On-going stress
◆ Physical health challenges

- ◆ Abuse or bullying
- ◆ Loss of a job or livelihood
- ◆ Prejudice
- ◆ Mental health challenges
- ◆ Marital or relationship issues
- ◆ Financial challenges
- ◆ Lack of opportunities
- ◆ Poor education

You may be familiar with some of these experiences, and you may also have experienced some difficulties that are not listed above. But the fact remains that the lack of self-confidence and low self-esteem is diminishing, both mentally and physically.

How to take control of your self-confidence and increase your self-esteem.

> "Self-esteem is made up primarily of two things: feeling lovable and feeling capable."
>
> ~Jack Canfield

If you lack confidence, and you have low self-esteem, I firmly believe you can do things that can increase your self-esteem and self-confidence. These traits are not genetic, and just as my friend Nick did, you don't have to work in synch with others to increase your self-confidence. If you think you're not competent, smart, attractive, brilliant, worthy, and beautiful, this can be changed. You can become worthy of respect and confidently go after your goals and dreams without thoughts of failure in the back of your mind. You can control your life by increasing your self-confidence and self-esteem and overcome negative emotions, such as the fear of failure by following the practical steps below. Now, this isn't a recipe, so you don't need to do everything discussed. Simply choose those that appeal to you. You can start with a few at first and try them, and if they work, you can incorporate some of the others. Build up the momentum from there.

Challenge your negative and inaccurate thoughts: You have to step up if you find yourself dwelling on only negative situations. Just like exercising and building muscles, you have to make a proactive decision to exercise your brain muscle by focusing more on the positive side of things. Moreover, your initial thoughts might not be the only way to view a situation, therefore, you need to vet your thinking process to identify other ways to solve the issue. You may need to ask yourself these questions: "Are my thoughts or perceptions consistent with available facts and logic?" "Are there other explanations for this situation?" These questions can help you challenge your harmful and inaccurate thoughts. Long-term negative thoughts and beliefs are sometimes tough to recognize, although many are actually just opinions or perceptions about a situation. Forgive yourself when you make mistakes and try not to jump towards a conclusion without properly thinking about several ways in with a situation might play out. Stay away from thinking patterns such as:

All-or-nothing thinking: People with this thinking pattern see things in two ways; for them, a situation is either good or bad. They believe in the principle of gain it all or lose it all. For example, they may say, "If I fail one out of my papers, then I'm a total failure." For them, there's no middle ground. It has to be a total pass or a total fail.

Mental filtering: People with this thinking process distort their views about a situation or a person by dwelling only on the negatives. They may say something like, "I made a mistake with the document, now I think I'm going to get fired."

Converting positives into negatives: People with this thinking pattern downplay their achievements and positive experiences. For example, they may say, "I only passed the bar exam because the exam was simple."

Jumping to a conclusion: People with this thinking pattern reach a negative conclusion very quickly with little or no evidence to support it. For example, they may say, "My girlfriend hasn't called me all day, so I must have done something to upset her."

Mistaking feelings for facts: People with this thinking process misunderstand their current short-term feelings for a long-term and permanent reality. For example, "I feel like a failure, therefore, I must be a failure."

Negative self-talk: People with this thinking pattern underestimate themselves with self-deceptive humor. For example, they may say, "You're loving and adorable. I don't deserve you. You'd be better off with someone who deserves you."

Take an inventory: If you are not sure how strong your self-esteem and self-confidence are, making a list of your personal qualities can help. If you find that you focus more on your weaknesses, that might be an indication that you are pushing yourself too hard, and maybe you need to calm down and consider a list of your achievements that will help you realize how far you've come. Consider your talents, abilities, and passion, and leave space for new future discoveries about yourself. Don't assume what you are right now is what you'll be like forever. Anticipate growth, and don't forget to put that into your inventory, too. People with high self-confidence levels leave a lot of room for daily and long-term improvement.

Acknowledge your success: Human beings are insatiable. We often dismiss or downplay our success as a product of mere luck or chance. Some might even dwell on a mistake they made, far after they have completed a project. However, people with high self-esteem celebrate their accomplishments, even if they did make mistakes when completing a project. They learn from their mistakes and aspire to do better in their future projects. They respect their peers and junior colleagues, and they respond with "thank you" whenever they are praised for their accomplishments rather than dismissing the praise they are given. People with self-confidence are neither arrogant nor narcissistic. Still, they have absolute confidence in their abilities to deliver when they are called upon to do. If they make mistakes when completing a project, they learn, apologize, and look for ways to progress rather than labeling themselves a *failure*.

"Be everything to you, not everything to everybody"

~Lisa Lieberman-Wang

Compare yourself with only yourself: In life, there will always be a bigger car, house, jet, or yacht. When you compare situations or things, there's always something bigger or smaller, and you will never win. Hence, the need to be comfortable with your own progress. You can't use other people's actions or inaction as a benchmark for self-esteem. In reality, there will always be someone who is better and more capable than you are in some areas of life. Research has shown that people who often compare themselves with their peers' achievement, as seen on social media, are more likely to suffer from low self-esteem. I would like to remind you that in most cases, what you see on most social media platforms isn't a projection of reality. People often share the best part of their life, and they hide anything that may appear inadequate or negative. What is best for others might not be best for you, therefore, you should make your own life the yardstick rather than other people's lives. So instead of comparing yourself with others, replace that habit with something more proactive and productive. Consider how far you've come with your life, business/work, and family. Compare yourself only with yourself, and let the focus be on you and not the other people. This is a great way to boost your self-confidence and increase your self-esteem.

Adjust your thoughts and believes: Replace your negative and inaccurate thoughts with reasonable and constructive thoughts using these strategies.

Avoid "must" and "should" statements: If you use these words while reflecting, you might be putting unnecessary pressure on yourself or others. A reduction in the use of these words can lead to more realistic expectations.

Use hopeful statements: Fall in love with who you are, while you work on yourself to become better daily. Also, treat yourself with kindness, and ultimately encourage yourself. You owe yourself that much because, in reality, nobody will love you like you will love yourself. For example, instead of thinking, *I might not do well in the presentation because I wasn't well-prepared*, instead, try thinking, *even though I wasn't adequately prepared, I can handle the situation.*

Forgive yourself: We all make mistakes. Moreover, our mistakes aren't a real reflection of who we are. Instead, they are an isolated moment in time. So, rather than beating yourself up over your mistakes, tell yourself, *yes, I made a mistake, but that doesn't make me a failure.*

Learn from your mistakes: Don't let your mistakes go to waste; make every mistake or failure an opportunity to learn. Ask yourself, *what can I do differently next time to stop this from happening again? What have I learned from this mistake that I could apply next time I'm doing something similar to get the best outcome?*

Re-label upsetting thoughts: You don't necessarily need to react to negative thoughts when they show up in your head. Instead, think of how you can channel your energy into discovering ways to become more proactive. In short, ask yourself what you can do to make the situation less complicated instead of being upset.

Encourage yourself: Always give yourself credit after achieving each milestone and also for how far you've come.

> "If you're searching for that one person that will change your life, take a look in the mirror."
>
> *~Unknown*

Practice self-care: The more you show that you value your own well-being, the more you will build up the capacity to love yourself. Pay attention to your body and mind. For example, stay away from food that can make you feel crabby or tired. Eating well, and exercising help you feel more optimistic about the future. As stated earlier in this book, exercise doesn't have to be intense. A daily run, walk, or jog will do. It would be best if you went for a stroll a couple of times each week, and you'll definitely see the benefits. Besides, spending more time with people who care about you may also help you care about yourself even more.

Take a brief self-appreciation break: This is an exceptionally straightforward and fun habit. If you follow through with this consistently for just one month, then it can have a significant effect on your mental health. This is how to go about it:

Take a full breath, slow down, and ask yourself this: *What are three things I value about myself?*

A couple of model examples that have come up when I have used this activity in the past include:

1. I help many individuals every day through what I create.
2. My work can make other people laugh and hopefully ignore their own problems.
3. I am incredibly mindful and caring with my pets.

These things don't need to be anything major. They can be as simple as you listening to someone who needed to get something off their mind. Or that you went for a quiet walk or bike ride after work as opposed to staying at home and watching TV. These brief breaks don't just have a positive impact on your confidence in the long run. In fact, these breaks can help you turn a negative mindset around, so that you experience a renewed sense of purpose and positive energy again.

Jot down three things at the end of each day that you can appreciate about yourself. Write your answers in your journal each night.

Another positive advantage of writing down your answers is that after some time, you can re-read them, so that you continue to remain positive, while also benefitting from a boost in self-confidence on the days when you need it the most.

Although the list above isn't revolutionary, it isn't comprehensive either. However, the good news is that you have a significant amount of control when it comes to boosting your self-confidence and self-esteem. These are simple, concrete, and practical steps that have helped Nick and I challenge our minds and bodies.

4.2 Resistance to Discomfort

> "If you are distressed by anything external, the pain is not due to the thing itself, but to your own estimate of it; and this you have the power to revoke at any moment."
>
> ~Marcus Aurelius

Analysts argue that humans are driven by two closely connected motivations: to stay happy and to avoid pain or discomfort. The majority of us dedicate more energy towards staying away from pain or discomfort. Rather than being proactive and making decisions that would lead to our own happiness, we respond to life's challenges by trying to escape or, worse yet, we waste energy fighting to limit our own discomfort. Rather than choosing to end a toxic relationship and, instead, pursue a better relationship, we may remain where we are, and either avoid confrontation or start one, so that we can ultimately feel a sense of control. Rather than leaving a horrible job to seek the one we love, we may remain where we are, only to complain about it constantly. Attempting to avoid discomfort all the time can be a problem, and it can also have real consequences.

As a child, who grew up in a motherless home, I felt consumed by pain. As a middle school student, I used food as a vehicle to avoid the pain. As a high schooler, I tried to starve the pain away. In college, I drank and smoked to cope with my painful reality. Also, in my twenties, I felt and cried my eyes out. I wailed. I wished I had never felt that way, yet I continued pushing the pain away, ignoring it, while also pretending everything was fine.

How to resist discomfort

The use of meditation to manage emotions can be effective.

> "The only thing that causes any kind of discomfort or pain is resistance to the natural self. So, the idea is to dig deep, find out what definitions, what beliefs you may be holding on to and still believing are true that are out of alignment with the reality that you prefer."
>
> ~ *Bashar*

It's so much simpler to manage emotions as they emerge, if you've consciously worked on yourself to the point where you have created a quiet inward space. In case you're new to meditating, you might need to attempt one of these straightforward approaches to make meditation simple and fun:

1. Take a look at your response to uncomfortable situations.

Most of the time, are you quick to judge someone else or a situation before you know all of the facts? Do you need someone else's compliments or approval in order to feel comfortable in your own skin? Do you accept how others feel about you and assume responsibility for that? Do you freak out in stressful situations, and blame everyone else around you? Are you too hard on yourself, and then end up feeling paralyzed when it comes to your own future potential?

2. Work on observing your own emotions and then take responsibility for them.

Sometimes, it is difficult to understand a feeling when it occurs, particularly if you feel you shouldn't be feeling that way. Unfortunately, these things happen. Rather than letting the discomfort get the best of you, attempt to pinpoint what you are feel in that moment. Are you frightened, disappointed, stressed, embarrassed, disturbed, or furious? Try to figure out exactly what the negative emotion is, and afterward, pinpoint what you think may be the reason for it. For example, your boss appeared to be upset with your work, so now you feel disappointed, or your spouse expressed their dissatisfaction with your attitude recently, so now you are mad at yourself for being so selfish. Whenever you feel uncomfortable about something you'd prefer to avoid, confront it head on by examining it as closely as possible in order to understand what caused it in the first place.

When you know exactly what you're feeling, this level of awareness will allow you to effectively challenge both the reason for it and, ultimately, its impact. You can ask yourself whether you're overreacting to the situation, or whether you're actually stressing over how to regain a sense of control. And afterward, you can decide to interpret the situation in another way, in order to relieve yourself, and ultimately feel something other than what you had expected. Nobody else is in charge of our emotions. Only we can choose to change them.

4.3 Developing the ability to predict your emotions in advance

The best way to predict your emotion is by creating it.

The term, *affective forecasting*, which means the ability to predict your emotions in advance, might be somewhat off-putting. All things considered, what on Earth does this even mean? Doesn't affective forecasting have something to do with climate change? Or, then again, maybe it's actually a measurable presentation of predicting sales for the next quarter? These exercises require clear engagement and, later, reflection.

Affective forecasting is developing an ability to predict your emotions in advance. It's the ability to predict how you will feel in the future. For reasons yet unknown, we often fail at knowing what will make us truly happy. Not to mention that we often find it difficult to look beyond the present moment, much less towards the future. Our emotions, in any given moment, can influence how we'll make choices later, in the future.

To simplify this concept even further, affective forecasting is a way to determine how a future situation or conflict – significant or not – will ultimately make you to feel.

A Brief History of Affective Forecasting

This concept was first characterized and then explored by specialists Timothy Wilson and Daniel Gilbert during the 1990s. Their interest was inspired by the idea that when we get what we need, we are not generally as satisfied as we thought we would be. This concept came about from the idea of wanting ultimate fulfillment. We anticipate that we will feel a sense of wholeness or completion (or satisfaction, relief, etc.) when we get what we truly need. This is at the core of *affective forecasting,* and shows how it can be a more effective method than the casual predictions we make about ourselves or the assumptions we make about what we're feeling.

This type of prediction isn't the same as trying to determine who will win the World Series, or whether the stock market will crash. As noted by the experts and their research on this subject, for the most part, *affective forecasting* started as an inquiry into our ability to predict our own reactions, as opposed to combining other people's perceptions with similar individuals' personal reactions. This has provided important data about how we predict and foresee our own future reactions. On the other hand, there's little proof in support or against this prediction. Lately, researchers have started to explore the reliability of our emotional reactions, in addition to the accuracy of our emotional predictions.

The Psychology of Affective Forecasting Theory

The early works of Gilbert, Wilson, and other scientists worldwide, have revealed the unpredictable and exciting ways that we can anticipate our future emotions, how we follow up on those expectations, and how often our predictions are right. Be that as it may, let's explore the foundation of affective forecasting. The foundation can be divided into four components.

The Components of *Affective Forecasting*

1. Uncertainty about how to characterize an emotion (i.e., "valence uncertainty"), regardless of whether the feeling will ultimately be positive or negative.
2. The type of emotion experienced.
3. The passion beneath the emotion.
4. The duration of the emotion.

When we try to anticipate our future feelings, we all, for the most part, consider whether those emotions will be positive (i.e., make us happier) or negative (i.e., make us sadder). We must also anticipate what explicit feeling(s) we will encounter, how strongly we will feel them, and how long they will last. Studies that have focused on these four components have, collectively, made a fascinating discovery — that the accuracy we, as individuals, predict about our own emotions can lead to each one of these four components changing fundamentally.

Examples of Affective Forecasting

Affective forecasting is something we do regularly throughout our daily lives. Every one of us, whether we realize it or not, make countless attempts to predict our own emotions.

If you're in doubt about the best way to predict your emotions, a psychological study suggests to assign one day just to notice all the times you anticipate your emotions about a future situation or event. Note each time you over-think/worry, and write down each instance. It may look something like this:

1. Anticipating a fun time at next Friday's happy hour.
2. Terrified of a visit to the dental specialist but hoping to feel less stressed out.

3. Feeling apprehensive about a meeting at work and expecting to feel restless and freaked out.
4. Impatient and nervous about the birth of our baby, but hoping to feel relieved, and happy after her birth.
5. Looking forward to meeting an old friend for espresso and maybe having a good time.
6. Expecting my old classmates to not even recognize me at the reunion. I'm hoping I won't feel humiliated and just want to go home.
7. I hope our football team wins their next game.

These are only a few of the many ways that we anticipate our future emotions every day.

How Affective Forecasting Impacts Happiness

It isn't difficult to understand how affective forecasting can impact our happiness. In other words, a significant portion of our happiness originates from predicting a positive event and dealing with our assumptions if there is a fall-out. For instance, an investigation of the 2020 political election between Donald Trump and Hilary Clinton found that Trump's supporters were typically optimistic about the potential for a win, while Hilary's supporters experienced hope, but, in the end, sadness because they obviously were not happy with the result of the election. In a situation where we overestimate how happy we will be after a future event, we will, in general, have a significant influence over how happy or sad we actually end up feeling. Then again, when we picture an upcoming and potentially positive event, we may feel even happier than we ever would have expected once the event is over.

Our attempt to predict how the future will impact our own happiness will be tested by significant (and, often, unpredictable) life events. We are so used to adjusting to change, in general, that the joy we experience from a single, positive event will only become a distant memory after a short period of time. If we are able to acknowledge this type of short-lived satisfaction for what it is, then we may try to hold on to that initial feeling of joy even longer. It's strange trying to figure out how to appreciate each moment for what it is, while also refusing to recognize that any single occasion alone could make our lives even better or, on the other hand, significantly worse.

Affective Forecasting and Decision-Making

Remember, when we discussed several situations where we could actually use affective forecasting in our everyday lives? How about we take those situations one step further:

- Because of the clear and specific expectations you have for your next getaway to be as perfect as possible, you have chosen to book yet another vacation even further into the future. This is something you most likely wouldn't have done if you weren't anticipating some sort of negative experience.

- You cancel your appointment with the dental specialist to avoid the pain and fear that you know, without a doubt, you'll feel at your appointment. This cancellation may have a clear, yet negative impact on your dental health.

- Anticipating that your morning espresso made you feel energized so that you chose to stop at a café every morning while on the way to work.

- In light of the company's annual meeting next week, you practice both your strengths and weaknesses, and even run mock meetings in order to feel as comfortable as possible. In the end, your preparation and composure will wind up helping you nail the meeting.

- Your eagerness to meet your new baby, motivates you to plan and design every possible twist and turn the birth experience may offer, and which may, in the long run, make you feel prepared.

- You are anticipating your espresso date so much that you choose to give them a small, yet thoughtful gift, which wins them over and is ultimately met with a mutually satisfying friendship.

- Because you are worried and stressed over what your old classmates will think of you, you choose to cancel the reunion a few days beforehand, therefore, upsetting your former classmates and consequently putting an end to the annual reunion once and for all (and maybe even your friendship with all of them, too).

These situations often consist of you making a decision about your actions based on your assumptions about a specific event in the future. Like most choices we make throughout our everyday lives, some of them lead to positive results, while some lead to negative results. The choices that lead to negative results are, more often than not, the after-effect of an imperfect situation. This can happen when any (or all) of the mistakes we had buried before re-surface.

There is no other area where it is more important to be mindful of our decision-making process than when choosing to understand genuine issues that relate to our own health. As indicated by analysts Halpern and Arnold (2008), there are three explicit systems that regularly influence a health-related dynamic:

1. **Focalism**: The emphasis on what will change instead of on what will remain constant.

2. **Immune neglect**: The inability to see how we can utilize our adapting aptitudes to address any despondency.

3. **Failure to anticipate change**: The inability to expect changes in our personal lives, and our overall capacity to adjust to these changes.

In case you're making an important decision about your health in the near future, be sure to remember these three issues.

Affective Forecasting and Social Interaction

As proposed in our rundown of *affective forecasting* above, there are countless social circumstances where emotional prediction may be beneficial. In general, we will have a pre-determined idea regarding how we will feel when hanging out with certain individuals. Spending time with those we love, the individuals who are motivating and elevating us frequently, will probably inspire positive feelings that will last a long time. While spending time with individuals we don't like can negatively impact us, predicting our desires for future emotions with people we don't know may have a similar effect. For example, high school students are likely going to feel bad or have a negative emotion, if they are told their favorite teacher has left the school, and a new teacher will be taking over. The students would, in general, rate their passionate response about this future situation significantly more negative than their experience actually was. This demonstrates that *affective forecasting* in a social context can be intensely affected by our need to concentrate on differences rather than similarities, even if there are unmistakably greater similarities than differences in a given situation.

Emotional Forecasting and Self-Regulation

At last, self-regulation is the final hybrid theme for *affective forecasting*. Anticipating our emotions can empower our ability to self-regulate. This is, to some degree, natural, especially when we have a slight idea of how we will feel later on or in the future. For example, if we know we will have a negative emotion in the future, we can prepare ourselves for it and work on facing the challenge head-on. If we know we may experience positive emotions in the future, we can work to embrace that feeling completely. This is particularly affirming for affective forecasting where the anticipated feeling is a positive one. On the other hand, anticipating negative feelings may make it progressively difficult to self-regulate, which can lead to foolish actions that can take us farther away from a potential solution.

However, anticipating a negative emotion can push you to be more enthusiastic, so that you strategically avoid any pointless, negative (and otherwise expected) results. Similarly, as with numerous other things in our everyday lives, our perspective can shape everything concerning our emotional anticipation and self-guidance.

4.4 Positive thinking

> "Train your mind to see the good in everything.
> Positivity is a choice, and the happiness in your life
> depends on the quality of your thoughts."
>
> *~Unknown*

The impact of positive thinking is a well-accepted idea, but every once in a while, it can feel a bit forced. Be that as it may, different scientific inquiries have noted the physical and mental advantages of positive thinking. A positive attitude can give you certainty, improve your state of mind, and even decrease the probability of developing adverse health conditions, such as depression, hypertension, and different stress-related health issues.

This may sound incredible, but what does it actually mean to be positive in both your thinking and in your actions? You can define positive thinking as positive symbolism, positive self-talk, or a general feeling of optimism or good faith. If you need to be consistently positive about every life situation, you'll need guidance to help you navigate that path.

Start each day on a positive note.

Create a habit where you start every day with something inspiring and positive. Here are a couple of examples:

- Tell yourself that it will be an extraordinary day or some other positive affirmation.

- Listen to an upbeat and positive song or playlist.

- Share some inspiration by offering a compliment or doing something nice for somebody else.

How you start your day establishes the pace for the rest of the day. Have you woken up late from the wrong side of the bed, and you're reluctant to even leave the house because you feel as if nothing good will happen for the rest of the day? You feel this way because you began the day with a negative feeling, and your skepticism has now affected the rest of your activities for the day. Rather than letting your current negative emotion overwhelm you, change your approach to the day by starting off on positive assertions. Regardless of how pointless it may seem, talk with yourself in the mirror, and make proclamations like, "Today will be a decent and fun-filled day," or "I will make the best use of today." You will be stunned by how much your day will improve.

> "If you don't like something, change it; if you can't change it, change the way you think about it."

> ~*Mary Engelbreit*

Concentrate on the good things.

Undoubtedly, you're going to experience obstacles on a daily basis. There's no such thing as a perfect day. When you experience such challenges, let your focus be on the good things, regardless of how minor or irrelevant those things may seem. For instance, if you arrive late to work as a result of heavy traffic, seize the moment and tune in to listen to your favorite radio station. Or if you visit your favorite restaurant and the chef tells you there are no more tables available, consider it an adventure to try a new restaurant.

Discover humor in terrible circumstances.

Give yourself permission to embrace humor in even the darkest or most difficult circumstances. Remind yourself that this circumstance will most likely make for a good story later, and it will be a great opportunity to make your friends laugh. Let's assume you got fired from work;

imagine the silliest way you could spend your final days at the office. Turning an otherwise terrible situation into a fun one doesn't necessarily mean you're not taking the situation seriously. Instead, it just shows you've decided to be at peace with yourself and everything around you that's out of your control.

Transform a disappointment into a life lesson.

Nobody is perfect. Undoubtedly, you will experience disappointment, in various settings, in numerous occupations, and with countless other individuals. Rather than blaming yourself for how you failed, consider what you will do next time. Transform your disappointment into a life lesson. Think about this in a concrete way. For instance, you could come up with seven new do's and don'ts for a new business based on your first business that failed.

Change negative self-talk into positive self-talk.

Negative self-talk is often difficult to notice because it's a gradual process. You may think you are terrible at babysitting or any other sensitive task, and you shouldn't have attempted it in the first place. However, this thought process will gradually transform into disguised feelings and might even negatively affect the way you see yourself. If your thoughts are always negative, you need to replace them with positive ones. For instance, change a statement such as, "I'm so terrible at this" to "With time I will get better; all I need to do is keep practicing." Convert every instance of negative self-talk into positive self-talk, and you will experience a gradual positive change in your perception and view about life.

Concentrate on the present.

Focus on today, this minute, and I mean there here and now! You may be getting reprimanded by your boss for what you did wrong last month, or your spouse is emotionally blackmailing you for the mistakes you made last year, and it's all gradually getting to you. Snap out of it and focus on the present moment. Concentrate on each second and not the future. Most of the time, what you're thinking is not as terrible as you have made it out to be. Most negative emotions come from memories of past events or some misrepresented fact about a situation that we cooked up in our heads. Always stay focused on the present moment.

Keep only positive friends, coaches, and colleagues in your circle.

When positive-minded individuals surround you, you will also experience uplifting perspectives, outlooks, positive stories, and positive assertions. Their positive outlook will rub off on you and influence your line of reasoning, which, at that point, will impact your outlook and, at the same time, lift the whole group's positive outlook. Surrounding yourself with only positive people can be daunting. However, you have to eliminate the negativity in your life before it consumes you. Do what you can to embrace the inspiration of others, and let their energy influence you.

Nearly anyone in any circumstance can apply these exercises to their own lives to increase their positivity. Positive thinking offers significant positive returns, so the more often you practice it, the greater the benefits you'll gain.

Section No. 5. Positive thinking is the key to a happy life.

5.1 Character traits that will help you cope with any problem

The truth of our character is expressed through the choice of our actions

We can all benefit from being more mindful of our personality and unique characteristics. This is because they are noteworthy indicators of our attitude and behavior. If you don't know what you want, simply settling, or trying to make the right decision at all can be unnerving. Understanding what makes us unique can prompt a more fulfilling life, better life decisions, and ultimately success in both our personal and professional circles. Everybody's defining character traits depend on their convictions, morals, ethics, and personality. Knowing your character traits can help you develop them further, and use them for your own benefit both in your professional life and in your personal relationships. Below are some of the character traits that can help you cope with any problem you will encounter as you continue to grow.

What are character traits?

Character is revealed when pressure is applied

Character traits are part of an individual's conduct or behavior, and they are recognized by the network and society around them. Also, they are often triggered in explicit circumstances.

For instance, think about your favorite hero in a book or film that you love. How does this individual react under pressure? How do they act when others around them are in a tough situation? The words you would use to describe them, such as *courageous*, *mindful*, or *fair*, are considered character traits or qualities. In new and difficult circumstances, some people buckle under tension, while others figure out how to just barely get by. To the contrary, there are some individuals who genuinely thrive in the face of personal challenges and misfortune. Fortunately, psychologists have come up with different individual character traits that will help us cope with our respective problems. When these character traits exist in combination, they can have a positive impact on an individual's chances of success.

Why are character traits essential in the working environment?

Habit changes into character

Mr. White is the senior business manager at Transcom Oil and Gas. He is happily married with two beautiful daughters, and he is well-respected among his colleagues and friends. At his 40th birthday party, his friend and colleague, James Smith, gave a toast. He described Mr. White as ambitious, passionate, creative, conscientious, courageous, flexible, honest, humble, honorable, loyal, honest, persistent, resilient, and disciplined. James smiled and raised his glass and said, "These are the unique characteristics that have helped us remain not only colleagues, but friends, and I also believe these character traits have helped you become the successful man you are today. Happy birthday, my dear friend."

Before you can develop your character traits, you must first identify them. The identification of your character traits will help you in your relationship and professional career. They will also help you with decision making that aligns with your personal and professional values. For instance, Mr. White was described as *creative, passionate, loyal*, and *honest* because people believe he takes his professional and marital life seriously. Besides, knowing your unique character traits will give you an edge over every other person who doesn't. It's important you identify your character traits as soon as you can — since doing so will set you apart from others who don't. Take, for example, your professional life. Your employer will always appreciate an employee who knows their character traits. Your unique traits are a valuable asset to an employer because it provides them with valuable information on how you will perform your job duties, manage stress, communicate with your colleagues, and manage high-pressure situations. For instance, when looking for people to manage a project, an employer may consider an employee with strong character traits such as those who are ambitious, disciplined, resilient, and persistent. This is because these particular character traits are indicative of someone who can manage or execute a project successfully.

Character traits that will help you cope with problems

Here are a few positive character traits that will be useful in not only your profession but also in your relationships. Determine whether you possess (or can relate to) any of the following traits. When you are aware of your best character traits, be sure to build on them, and always use them to your advantage.

Ambitious: An ambitious individual is someone who wants to make progress by accomplishing their goals. You may exhibit ambition when you are hardworking and dedicated to advancing your career and achieving your personal and professional goals.

Creative: Creative individuals often think outside of the box — whether that means creating a new, innovative solution to a problem or crafting a new invention. Innovation or creativity doesn't just apply to artistic jobs, either. Creativity can be used in every professional sector to solve difficult or challenging situations, present a complicated case in a simpler way, or even by completing a task by using the easiest method possible. Creativity is always necessary to solve a problem as quickly and as efficiently as possible.

Compassionate: A caring individual is someone who can both feel and express compassion toward others. You may show empathy when you help a co-worker conquer a difficult or trying situation. Likewise, sympathy is a useful quality in any position, and it can be especially valuable in customer-care roles.

Enthusiastic: Enthusiasm is infectious. The truth is, if you don't believe in yourself, other people won't either. Therefore, you have to be enthusiastic about every situation. Staying happy even when you're going through a terrible situation could even help you manage mental illness. More importantly, it doesn't cost you anything to stay happy, but it can cost you everything if you're not.

Curious: When you're curious, you are always inquiring *why*. This is because you're curious to know more about something. Also, you're never afraid to try different things in new and innovative ways. You may frequently ask, "What can I do to improve the situation?; or How can I improve at this?" If you possess this type of mindset, you're the *curious* type. Curiosity often leads to innovation, so I will advise you to keep building on it and always look for ways to improve.

Sense of urgency: A sense of urgency is critical for success because without it, you may never complete a task. Even when you put in a little bit of effort, you will often think about why you *can't* do it. Instead, think less and focus on accomplishing more. In my business, I frequently tell employees, "Without a sense of urgency, we can't achieve our goals." Therefore, in order to overcome challenges, we have to pursue our goals with a great sense of urgency.

Momentum: Make sure you do everything in your power to stay inspired. Experiencing a lack of momentum can be demoralizing. Momentum not only keeps you energized to do the work ahead, but it can also impact the productivity of the people around you. Do what you need to do to keep things moving. Don't wait until the end of the day to respond to an e-mail. Whenever you have a missed call from someone you need to talk to, don't wait until later to return their call. When your momentum is maximized, your team momentum is also maximized, and there will hardly be any problem you can't tackle. And while it's important to keep your momentum high and on target, don't be the reason other people are experiencing low level of momentum.

Focus: When you understand what you're trying to achieve and how you're going to achieve it, coping with difficult situations can become easier because your eyes are on the end goal, and you understand whatever you're going through at the moment won't last.

Empathy: Try not to dismiss what's important to somebody else. Before you react, try to consider every possible outcome of your actions. Put yourself in the other person's shoes. We are all human, and you need to be in the other person's position to fully understand their situation. Don't be in a rush to make decisions based on the current circumstances. Take your time, and think about the effect of your actions on the other person before making a move.

Self-control: Things can always turn out badly. Building up the capacity to weather a storm calmly without going overboard will help you cope effectively with a problem. It is important to keep your composure when faced with challenges, and think of ways to mitigate the effects; losing control will only further compound the problem. Therefore, to cope during a difficult situation, get a grip on your emotions, and stay composed while working out ways to solve the problem.

Courageous: A courageous person is somebody who isn't thrown off by difficulties and challenges. They're probably going to take on new ventures all the time that other people consider excessively difficult or time-consuming. Likewise, they may face more unique challenges in their work environment, which can increase the organization's revenue and productivity.

Adaptable: Adaptable individuals can rapidly adjust to changes in plans. For example, they can acclimate to the needs of new customers, etc. The capacity to change your behavior in order to suit your current situation will largely help you cope with difficult situations in the future.

Honest: A genuine individual is consistently honest and, for the most part, doesn't feel comfortable engaging in unethical practices. While honesty is fundamental in all positions, it's particularly significant in vigorously managed enterprises, such as social insurance, etc.

Humility: Humble individuals practice humility at a superior level. They don't boast about their achievements, and when they are praised for their success, they make sure they acknowledge the contributions of other people. For instance, when a humble boss gets an award for their achievement, they make sure every member of the team is also recognized, and they may even dedicate the award to the other team members.

Faithful: A loyal person is always faithful to their cause. They are committed and truthful in everything they do. Loyal people stay true to their organization, marriage, relationships, and all of their commitments. Faithful people can be trusted with vital information. The ability to stay true to what you are committed to will ultimately help you stay out of trouble.

Patience: Patience is the greatest of all virtues. A patient person can withstand setbacks, delays, or sudden difficulties without becoming frustrated or furious. Patience is also very important in a relationship. Remember, a relationship is made up of two people with different upbringings and ideologies. Therefore, there will always be misunderstandings and disagreements in most relationships. But if you're patient, there will be less room for fighting and more room for productivity. At work, your colleagues or boss may get on your nerves, but patience will help you control the situation without blowing things out of proportion. When dealing with others, we all need a lot of patience to help us mitigate the negative effects of fights or misunderstandings.

Perseverance: People who are persistent relentlessly pursue their objectives. They proceed with their way despite any impediments or troubles they may face along the way. Challenges and difficulties will always arise in your relationships and profession, but you will always win if you can persevere anyway.

Resilient: A resilient person is a tough individual who can rapidly recover from difficulties, stress, circumstances that aren't ideal, or any sudden changes in a situation. For instance, when you fail to meet a target, don't just sit back and give up. Start all over again but this time, consider what you've learned from your recent failure and make a better plan. Resilient people don't dwell on their failures; they learn from their mistakes and start over. You may fail, but don't simply stop at failure.

Discipline: In a relationship hierarchy, I think discipline should come right after love in terms of importance. Discipline is also a great virtue. It will help you overcome temptations in your relationship, and it will also help you resist the urge to get involved in inappropriate behavior at work.

Everyone ought to know their own characteristic traits, and if you don't, follow the listed traits and look for the ones that are similar to your character and personality. Characteristic traits, when properly developed and channeled in the right direction, will help you cope with most problems in every area of your life.

5.2 How to handle other people's aggressive behavior

Dealing with people's aggressive behavior can be daunting, confusing, and disturbing, especially if you have a close relationship with someone who is aggressive. But suppose you are armed with some useful information about how anger and other aggressive behavior really works. In that case, you will be able to manage yourself effectively and also manage the impact of the other person's anger.

Anger and aggression

Anger is the emotion we feel when people act or do things we don't like. In contrast, aggression is the act of expressing our anger through actions or words. Anger is an emotion, while aggression is an action, and there has to be anger before we can have aggression. In most cases, people aren't afraid of other people's anger, but they are terrified by the consequences or aftermath of their aggression.

Aggression may lead to:
◆ Insults
◆ Shouting
◆ Any form of aggressive speech
◆ Physical abuse

163

◆ Physical altercations

◆ Anxiety

◆ Fear

◆ Loneliness

◆ Guilt

When someone close to you or your spouse gets angry and starts to throw tantrums to attract outside attention, most people who find themselves in such a situation would usually handle it in one of two ways:

1. **Attack back by getting aggressive**

They shout back at the aggressor, and they both keep going back and forth until some kind of resolution has been reached. Unfortunately, this only makes the situation worse because the aggressor may become even more out of control and feel the need to throw more aggressive tantrums.

2. **They ignore the behavior or give in**

Some people are simply not built for trouble. They have little or no tolerance for confrontation because they are afraid of escalating anger and aggression. Instead of fighting or shouting back at their aggressor, this type of person would ignore, give in, tolerate, or even apologize for another person's aggression. Unfortunately, this type of response will only reinforce and justify the other person's behavior and allow the same scenario to repeat itself in the future.

Ideal ways to deal with another person's aggression

Wayne and Bullock have been living together for over two years. Although they are not officially married, they seem to be a perfect couple. However, things changed after Wayne lost his job at the coal factory. He became an alcoholic, and he gradually became a shadow of himself. Bullock had to step up to take responsibility for paying the rent and providing food for the household. She was hoping Wayne would snap out of his drunken stupor and get a new job, but Wayne wasn't showing any interest in doing that. His excuse was either the new job would be too stressful, too far away, or that the health insurance would be inadequate. Wayne frequently becomes aggressive towards the Bullock, and he often shouts at her on a daily basis, although she claims he doesn't hit her. Each time she returns home from work, she would complain to him about how much she hates his recent behavior. But Wayne always becomes defensive, before criticizing everyone except himself for his new circumstances.

How should Bullock respond?

First, Bullock should start by validating Wayne's anger and frustration. She might tell him:

"I know how it feels losing your job, and I know it sounds like I'm criticizing you, but I'm not. I just want a better life for both of us. A life where we if we want something, then would be able to raise money to buy it together. But we can't do that if you're not working. I know you are a great man who cares for me, but I'm struggling with paying the rent and feeding both of us. I need some help and you getting a new job will give me that."

Bullock was able to make her point without shouting back at Wayne, and this makes it less likely that Wayne would spiral into a rage in his own defense. He knows she needs support, so it's only right that he gets a job. But a reasonable resolution won't happen if Wayne disregards her words and, instead, says:

"This is bullshit! You're just trying to make me feel guilty. I could do all you're doing now and more if the government acted right. You're just lazy."

This is an example of aggression and Bullock needs to set clear boundaries to avoid further altercations with him.

Here's how to get started:

- Be clear about your definition of aggression and state what you will and won't tolerate. You may need to write them down.

- Determine what would be your point of action if such a situation repeats itself in the future. For example, Bullock may say, "If Wayne criticizes me, I'm going to ask him to stop immediately, and if he doesn't, I will just walk out."

- Be tough when setting boundaries, but try to avoid meeting the other person's aggression with your own anger. Follow your own rules. The other person's response to your decision might not be easy. Don't feel guilty about that; you're not responsible for fixing their problems.

- When the other person is calm, let them know their aggression is an issue, and that you need them to work on it. Make sure you tell them this on a day they are visibly calm because if you tell them at the wrong time, you may only make them angrier. Let them know your position and be sure to set boundaries for their aggression and how you feel they should handle a similar situation in the future.

On the other hand, if the aggression is beyond your control or your safety is at risk, it's advisable to seek professional help or call the police. You can also see a therapist or counselor for further advice.

5.3 How to quickly reduce emotional stress

> "Stress can destroy much more than just our physical health; too often, it eats away your hope, beliefs, and faith."
>
> ~Charles F. Glassman

Everybody feels worried at some point. Sometimes, you may even feel greater emotional stress than you're used to. Emotional stress is the stress which tends to disturb your natural equilibrium or any circumstance that will, in general, upset the harmony between a living thing and its environment. What separates our level of stress tolerance is the degree to which stress influences your daily life, and the strategies you adopt in order to deal with it. Generally speaking, it's almost impossible to avoid emotional tension or stress situations, but we can learn to manage them in order to keep them from damaging our health and robbing us of our happiness.

How to reduce emotional stress

> "Doing something productive is a great way to alleviate emotional stress. Get your mind doing something that is productive."
>
> ~ Ziggy Marley

As discussed earlier, you can't eliminate stress from your life, but you can learn to manage it. The stress management strategies listed below will help you cope with frequent amounts of emotional stress. These may include:

- **Finding a hobby that helps you unwind**

Everybody needs personal time to unwind and blow off the steam that comes with emotional stress. Your hobby might be exercising, watching a movie, reading, listening to music, or simply walking your pet. Just do whatever makes you happy to ease those stressful moments. Don't downplay the importance of how unwinding can reduce your emotional stress levels.

- **Avoiding foods that trigger emotional stress**

Sensitive food, such as sugar, gluten, milk products, or processed food can influence your mood. This class of food contains some components that can significantly impact your mood. For example, sugar and glucose can make you feel either full of energy or left with a sugar crash. Avoid these foods and consume more natural whole foods in order to stay healthy.

- **Get consistent sleep**

When you're sleep deprived or when your sleeping quality is poor, you are vulnerable to higher levels of emotional stress. That's bad for your health. Regardless of how busy your schedule may be, make sure you get at least six hours of uninterrupted sleep daily. Getting a good night's rest is one of the easiest things you can do to improve your emotional well-being.

- **Take control of the situation**

Individuals who remain in charge of their circumstances, are less worried or emotionally stressed than those who are not in control. Taking control of a situation means doing all you can to improve your mental and physical health, so that you stop worrying about what you can't control.

- **Write them down**

Stressing over your circumstances can only intensify your emotional stress. Writing down how you're feeling can help release those negative emotions. Being expressive with our emotions is an effective way of reducing anxiety.

- **Make use of anxiety-easing tools**

Make use of tools that can help you ease the stress you are feeling. Tools, such as popular apps on our smartphones can be of great help. There are a lot of apps you can download to help you ease your tension. You just need to find out which one will be the most effective for you and then download it. Many of these apps are free, so research a few of them and determine whether they will work for you.

- **Make use of stress-management strategies**

Stress-management strategies, such as deep breathing, meditation, yoga, and changing your "thinking processes" are effective strategies that can help you manage your emotional stress. Although these strategies don't work like rocket science, they take time and practice before they begin to have a serious impact on your stress level. You have to stay committed and put in the required work before you begin to see changes in your general well-being.

The tips or steps above are not meant to replace the advice of your physician. If you are struggling with emotional stress, it's advisable to seek medication, therapy, or consult your physician. Talk to a therapist; they can help you reduce your emotional stress by talking you through your emotional baggage.

5.4 Methods that will help you regain control

When we feel offended or cheated, it's very easy to lose our sense of self-control. When you lose control over your emotions in a tense situation, you may also discover you've ultimately lost your patience. However, if you can figure out how your emotions work, you will be able to have better control over a situation without losing total self-control. Once you learn how to control your emotions, you will find it easy to keep your mind on whatever you might want to accomplish because you are now in charge. Your success and failure, to a large extent, is tied to your habits. However, success is often only built on good habits, and good habits are built on discipline, discretion, and by eliminating bad habits. Therefore, if you want to be at the top of your game, you will need to learn how to keep yourself in control, and this can only be achieved through physical and mental discipline.

A great man once said, "self-control is one of the most daunting daily tasks," and I couldn't agree more. This is obvious in how we can sometimes disregard our daily goals, such as consuming fewer calories, or failing to study until the night before the test as opposed to studying the material throughout the semester. The motivation behind why it is so hard to control our calorie consumption, or for a student to refusal to prepare for an exam well in advance is because we lack self-control. If you find yourself in a similar position, then you'll need to take back your life by regaining control by using the steps below.

Cole's physician has told him that he weighs more than he should, and therefore, he needs to reduce his calorie consumption and increase his physical activity every day. Cole understands the severity of the situation, so he has realized that he has no other choice than to follow his physician's advice. However, Cole is addicted to cakes, and his problem just got bigger because his friends are also cake fans, too, and each time they visit a café or restaurant, they all over-indulge in cake. In those moments, Cole often thinks to himself, "it's just a piece of cake; it won't hurt," so he joins his friends and overindulges in his favorite dessert. How can he practice self-control in the face of ultimate temptation?

Jane is divorced, and she's the mother of two boys. Jane works at one of the fast-food joints in town, and she makes just enough money to take care of herself and her kids. She's a serial cigarette smoker, too. However, each time she quits, she always returns to smoking within a few months. She's worried about the impact of smoking on her health, however, each night she tells herself, "It's just a stick of cigarette; it won't hurt," then she goes ahead and smokes anyway. What can Cole and Jane do to take regain control of their situations?

Jane and Cole are both suffering from *Dual-motive conflict.* This is a psychological term used to represent a situation when an individual has to choose between two opposing objectives, such as following a diet vs. wanting cake or quitting smoking vs. smoking anyway. From the example above, it's obvious Cole knows his health is at risk, and he also knows he can't lose his excess weight by avoiding a single piece of cake. Losing weight takes a lot of time, dedication, and hard work, so eating just one piece of cake may not necessarily endanger Cole's health, and since he's always happy at the sight of cake, he indulges himself with it. But in the long run, this behavior is dangerous to his health.

Simple steps to help you regain control.

● Tell people about your goals

Let's assume Cole told his friends that his physician told him his health was at risk, and that he must go on a strict diet. Therefore, he can no longer join them to eat cake at the café. Telling his friends about his plan will strengthen his friendship with them, have a positive impact on his diet plan, and put him in better control of his health.

● Remain focused on your goals

Setting a reminder, jotting down your goals, and displaying those goals around your room and on the homepage of all your tech. devices can help you create a visual reminder of why you need to stay on your goals. One major issue with long-term goals, however, is that their outcomes are not always visible at the beginning of the process. However, recording your goals and visualizing them will help you stay true to your goals and ultimately help you remain in control.

● Measure Your Progress

Measurement is meant to help you appreciate how far you've come, and if you need to put in more work. Measuring your progress keeps you focused on your objectives.

● Avoid Temptation

Sometimes the best thing you can do to maintain control of your actions is to avoid temptation altogether. For instance, if you are on a diet, it's best to avoid food-related pictures, movies, places, or friends that might trigger your hunger for what you're craving/avoiding. Just like Cole, if you don't want to eat cake, avoid the café or bakery. Since many people often give in to temptation, the best way to regain control in such a situation is avoidance. Don't try to go there and say *no* when you're face-to-face with the very thing you've been avoiding. It's better not to test yourself and push yourself to the limit when you know you're likely to break. Stay in control by avoiding these situations altogether.

- **Prioritize your goals**

It is very easy to lose sight of a goal when it isn't a priority. Generally speaking, any task can be difficult, and we sometimes find it difficult to continue, especially when we do not see an immediate result. However, you need to maintain control by prioritizing your goals. That's the only way you'll get motivated to wake up in the morning for exercise or avoid smoking and excessive food consumption. Make a daily schedule and mark each day that you achieved your goal. Make sure you stay committed to the goal by prioritizing it.

- **Learn How to Manage Stress**

Stopping to take a couple of deep breaths will enable your heart rate to slow down. This practice will help you relax for a short amount of time. Manage stress by exercising regularly, eating a healthy diet, and getting enough sleep. When you manage your stress level effectively, you will be focused, sleep well, and make rational decisions. Figuring out how to manage your stress in a healthy way will ensure you are mentally and physically fit for tackle your daily tasks.

- **Forgive Yourself**

> "Success consists of going from failure to failure
> without loss of enthusiasm."
>
> ~*Winston Churchill*

You will burn out at some point because coming up short is simply a normal part of life. forgive yourself and move on. Dwelling on your mistakes won't change anything. But you can always learn from your mistakes. As discussed earlier in this book, your habits and attitudes will determine your success. Keep yourself in control by forgiving yourself and moving on towards a happier and healthier version of yourself. At the same time, don't forget to hold on to the valuable lessons you learned from both your negative and positive experiences.

It's easy to control your emotions, actions, habits, and attitude when you decide to follow and commit to the points made above. Stay true to yourself, and follow these steps in order to keep yourself in control.

Conclusion

In this book, we have identified several different negative emotions, and how they can interfere with our success or personal growth if they're left unchecked. Negative emotions are part of our daily life, and therefore, there's no way to avoid them. We have to learn how to control them from spinning out of control. We have explained negative emotions comprehensively, and how they can be controlled by using simple, practicable behavioral exercises in the context of several real-life experiences and motivational quotes. This book will help you overcome your challenges with negative emotions. Thereby helping you have more control over the emotions that affect your relationships in both your personal and professional life. The methods used in this book are flexible and applicable to anyone who is willing to take back control of their life.

This material contains a lot of real-life, relatable examples that highlight how we can manage our negative emotions with a specific focus on anger in the third chapter. This is despite the fact that anger is actually a sub-category of negative behavior, and has caused countless difficulties for many people. Anger, as we have seen, has played a vital role in human evolution, including helping us express ourselves when words can sometimes fail us. However, when misunderstood and misdirected, anger can cause significant damage, both for the person with the anger and everyone else around them. When left untreated, explosive anger can cause a wide range of social and economic problems for individuals and society, in general.

This book also discusses other aspects of negative emotion, which include fear, disgust, surprise, happiness, and sadness. We have extensively explored the origin of negative emotion in order to understand its origin. We recommend approaching your negative emotions in a mature and methodical manner, like the approaches outlined in this book, in order to maximize your chances of taking total control of your emotions. These approaches recognize the power of these emotions, the reasons they exist, the responsibilities associated with them, and the difficulties they can cause both for the person with the emotion and everyone else in their life. However, the approaches outlined in this book are not meant to replace your doctor's advice, but, in fact, they may compliment your doctor's advice and help you stay happy and, ultimately healthy.

Life has a way of bringing out the worst in everyone, but with the practicable methods and techniques used in this book, you'll learn how to embrace your weaknesses and transform them into your strengths. Your emotions will no longer control you because now *you're* in charge. We all need help managing our emotions from time to time, and I think following the methods detailed in this book is a great way to get started. I'm happy you purchased this book, and I'm even happier I was able to help you along on your journey. Continue improving, and never stop searching for what will make you happy. Take control of your life today!